7/11/19

For
Scott

WEALTHBEING

A Guide to Creating Wealth and Enjoying Wellbeing

Malcom

MALCOLM DURHAM

RedDoor

'At last a book that acknowledges the importance of both emotional and financial fulfilment and explains how they can go hand in hand. It is also packed full of hard won knowledge from Durham and practical advice for following in his footsteps. Leaves you energised and empowered.'

Andrew G. Marshall, marital therapist and author of *Wake Up and Change Your Life: How to survive a crisis and be stronger, wiser and happier*

'WealthBeing is an essential guide for anyone who is thinking of creating some wealth but is not sure of the challenges to their wellbeing that this might entail. The practical, accessible real-life stories and clear financial examples, will reassure anyone who is determined to make a difference and feel fulfilled as a result.'

Duncan Cheatle, Founder of Prelude Group, home to The Supper Club, Britain's premier club for fast-growth founders and CEOs and Founder of RiseTo, an online platform that improves employability in young people.

'A good read that covers what really matters for entrepreneurs. Malcolm has reflected honestly on his own journey and has offered us that same flat mirror with sage learnings, tips, tools and templates. It's not so much about the money; more about feeling that your success was worthwhile.'

David Glassman, *Coach and mentor to successful business leaders*

'I always choose mentors that have been there, done that, got the t-shirt, and in the wealth world Malcolm Durham ticks those boxes and it is an honour to call him a friend. But unlike so many other "Wealth Gurus" out there, Malcolm recognises the full integration of wealth and BEING, wealth on its own is hollow... a must read for anyone serious about wealth and life, I choose BOTH ;-).'

Deri Llewellyn-Davies AKA 'The Strategy Man'

FOREWORD

The value of having a wealth plan, or at least knowledge of how money works in school and in adult life, is sadly missing. Wealth for me is not all about money. For me money is a scorecard of my success to some extent, indeed making enough money not to have to think about money was a major goal as I built and ran my business but the reason for the money need was twofold.

1. I wanted to be able to afford the best education possible for my children, as my parents had afforded me. I think that this is an esteem issue as well as perhaps an upbringing influence.

2. I saw money as 'freedom' in every way possible and always was aware that money cannot buy happiness as often people seem to think.

For that you need a wellbeing plan. For me the value of an individual really getting to grips with their own needs, goals and aims and the value of the different desires in life is so significant that I think it should be taught in the early years of schooling.

In *WealthBeing* Malcolm has offered some simple, easy to follow thinking and well-designed tools to deliver a change in understanding wealth and wellbeing. Like all great things, start with the mindset and anything is possible. Enjoy this book, but remember, it is sod all use without application.

Lara Morgan
Motivational speaker, mentor and author, founder of Pacific Direct,
Chief Growth Accelerator at Company Shortcuts, which is transforming
the way entrepreneurs and growth leaders are educated and supported.

CONTENTS

1 Introduction   8

2 Creating it   38

3 Launching it   70

4 Nurturing it   100

1

INTRODUCTION

WealthBeing and me

Thank you for taking the time to read this guide to creating wealth and enjoying a sense of wellbeing.

I believe we have moved beyond the old focus on work–life balance. These days many people want two things in their lives:

1. A reasonable amount of wealth, and the freedom that it brings.

2. A feeling of wellbeing, with the knowledge that they have fulfilled their emotional needs, and can continue to do so.

The problem is that it always looks like a trade-off. The usual ways of achieving one always seem to involve giving up on the other.

On the WEALTH side

If you're aiming for the top of the corporate tree as a route to financial independence, the perceived wisdom is that this will mean working long hours over many years and sacrificing the joys of family life. Virtue is not always rewarded, success is not guaranteed and the commitment required may take a physical toll.

If you create your own business, the rewards can be greater and you probably won't get fired. But you may need to give up a career and risk savings built up over years in a venture that could fail in weeks, destroying your finances and your self-esteem.

On the WELLBEING side

The quest for emotional fulfilment may demand even more than the ambition for wealth. I've seen advice that says you should spend six hours a day communicating with others. Nice work, if you can get it. The pundits offer nothing about how to hold down a job at the same time.

People who make a real commitment to fulfilling their emotional needs often become disillusioned with the world we live in. They may be left stuck in the middle – unhappy with society's insistent materialism, but feeling empty when they reject it.

So what can we do? The answer – or, at least, one answer – is WealthBeing.

WealthBeing is a way of creating wealth and nurturing your wellbeing, without having to choose one at the expense of the other. It's a way of having the pounds without the pain. It's a way of combining the two in a uniquely satisfying state of balanced contentment. It's a way of achieving, if not nirvana, at least what one of my friends (a big fan of Winnie the Pooh) insists on calling 'plentifitudleness'.

This isn't the right path for everyone. But I believe it is a path many people would love to follow, if only they could see where it is. There have been plenty of books on wealth creation and lots more on wellbeing. But up till now there's been nothing, as far as I can see, that brings them both together. After all, how are you supposed to follow a wealth creation guide that asks you to commit to keeping your customers happy 24/7, if you're also being told you must spend six hours a day socialising and communicating with those around you to nourish your wellbeing?

> WealthBeing is a way of creating wealth and nurturing your wellbeing, without having to choose one at the expense of the other

This book is aimed at solving this conundrum. Its goal is to draw together the essential elements of business and wellbeing in a practical guide based on my own experience and on what I have learned from hard knocks and wise heads along the way.

WealthBeing is a combination of financial freedom, which allows me to do what I choose to do, and the satisfying feeling that my emotional needs have been met. I'm not famous and I don't own a football club, a Ferrari or any of the other trappings that bolster the egos of wealthy men. What I do have – most of the time – is a sense of deep contentment, of having a life that has value, both financially and emotionally, to me and to others. I am in a position where I am able to do the things I enjoy, either for myself or because they benefit others (while always being small, in the general scheme of things). Like all states of life, it's not permanent. But if you know what to do, you can create and maintain it.

One way I can help others is by passing on what I have learnt, to help them create WealthBeing too. The road that's brought me here has included its fair share of trials and tribulations, including depression, divorce and various other setbacks and disasters. You won't necessarily have to struggle with those particular problems, but it is inevitable that you, too, will find that things happen to you, from time to time, which you would much prefer to avoid. That's where guides are useful. Whether you're reading a book or picking someone else's brains, they can help you avoid the pitfalls, or help you climb back out of them when you haven't managed to dodge the forces of darkness.

I've used guides, too. They didn't save me from getting things wrong, but they did help me get out of trouble. This book shares the principles which I relied on (and still do), such as those highlighted in Stephen R Covey's *The 7 Habits of Highly Effective People* and in less well-known books such as Susan Scott's *Fierce Conversations*, alongside my own tips and experiences. Together they can be applied to help you achieve 'plentifitudleness', balance and WealthBeing.

My road to WealthBeing

In July 1989, my father died, at the age of 56, and I took over as non-executive chairman of our family's business, Gordon Durham & Co.

Gordon Durham & Co was a building contractor in the Northeast of England with sales of around £5 million and a good reputation among the councils and housing associations it worked with. I was only 28, but as the finance director of a public company I already knew enough to take on the role. My first tasks were to slash bank borrowings of £800,000 – equal to our total net assets – and to fight off a £400,000 claim against us from a former business partner who said he was entitled to a large share of the profits from a recent office block development. It was a bruising baptism of fire that lasted three years, after which we were ordered to pay him £75,000. But he wasn't satisfied, mounting an unsuccessful appeal against the award and then trying, unsuccessfully, to take the case to the House of Lords.

The complicated situation I found myself in meant I quickly learnt a lot about the harsh realities of business, families and the law. The directors of Gordon Durham & Co were at odds with each other, as one of them was a friend of the plaintiff and my mother and brother were so involved in dealing with my father's death that they had little energy to spare. The whole experience was educational, rather than enjoyable, and it left me wondering whether this was really what I wanted to do with my life.

I needed more control over what was happening around me, and it was my beloved Uncle Drew who put his finger on the nub of the problem. 'You'd be a lot happier if you were running your own business, Malcolm,' he said. I tried the corporate life again as FD of another plc, but soon realised the wisdom of his words and set about starting my own company, providing my services as a part-time FD to small- and medium-sized enterprises. Though our first child was on the way, my wife backed this move to a less certain existence and the company that is now known as Flexible Directors was born as FD Solutions.

For most of the 1990s, Gordon Durham & Co made hardly any profits at all and FD Solutions had mixed fortunes. Engagements were hard to secure and while I had a loyal partner, Richard Brooks, to support me, I also bumped into a number of negative or dishonest people who broke contracts, failed to pay their bills and even threatened me with disqualification as a chartered accountant. This was an empty threat, but it upset me a lot at the time. I was shocked at how greedy and malicious these people I'd trusted could be. One of these 'ungentlemen' is now worth £100 million+ and another is currently an MP.

It was a depressing experience, and I duly became depressed. It took a fair bit of medical support and guidance from Adrian Gilpin, a leadership and emotional intelligence guru, to give me a measure of control over my emotional state.

Then the good stuff started to happen. In the mid-90s, D:Ream sang (and Tony Blair 'sang') 'Things Can Only Get Better' and soon afterwards they did. I started managing my emotional state and forming good relationships with capable people who believed in creating something and sharing it, rather than fighting for the largest slice of the cake. There are two ways of achieving wealth – you can take it *from* others or create it *with* others – and WealthBeing, of course, is firmly based on the latter. As times got easier, both the businesses began to get a lot more work and it kept on rolling in, year after year. Eventually, in May 2006, I received a call from Brendan Farrell, a broker who helps people buy and sell construction companies. Brendan asked me straight out how much I wanted for Gordon Durham & Co, and I replied, equally straight out, '£10 million.'

'Ah, right. OK. £10 million, eh?' he said, clearly thinking this was crazy talk. 'And where would you like the cheque?'

But he didn't put the phone down. I had my spreadsheets to show how I had arrived at this figure and I was sticking to my guns, so he agreed to see what he could do. Some months later, he got us an offer from a venture capital firm for £8.5 million, which was quickly bumped up to, yes, £10 million. My past experience with my family and the directors of Gordon Durham & Co had led me to keep these negotiations confidential so the news came as quite a shock to them. When I asked them to consider it and see what they thought, their reactions amazed me. The directors, who would each get half a million pounds and a continuing stake in the business, wouldn't entertain the idea of selling to venture capitalists, and my relatives, advised by an old friend of my father's, called for a family conference.

This conference opened with the old friend expressing the family's dissatisfaction with my 18 years as chairman. Ignoring the fact that we had narrowly avoided insolvency when I took over and now had an offer that would make us all a lot of money, he focused his attack on three investments I had made, totalling £75,000, and the purchase of a yacht. I'd bought the boat as a corporate asset, with the idea that we could use it for training and entertaining. But I was wrong. It looked too much like an executive toy. It was a mistake to buy it, so we agreed that I should, effectively, buy it. The investments in shares, though, were perfectly justifiable – we'd made some handsome profits in the past and they represented only a small proportion of our assets. Even if the current holdings were worthless, they would not stop us trading (and one of them actually made a profit of 400%).

I had the choice of fight or flight – and I fled briefly, realising that the fight option would destroy what I had built and was aiming for. Flight gave me five minutes to compose myself and apply what I had learned about protecting my own wellbeing. I went back to the meeting and started working towards my long-term goal – WealthBeing.

And here's the point of the story. As I listened to the petty complaints, accompanied by plans to place new restrictions on my future activities, I realised how much progress I'd made in the previous few years. By practising what I had learnt, seeing its rewards and refining it here and there, I had developed the ability to rise above any angry reactions that would have clouded my judgement, even under extreme provocation. I was able to stay in control. I could make conscious choices, reacting calmly, managing my emotions and staying firmly focused on my aim of selling Gordon Durham & Co for a life-changing amount of money.

But if a deal with the venture capitalists was out of the question, who could we sell it to?

It was the managing director of GD, the one outsider who had unexpectedly been invited to this family conference, who came up with the solution. He wouldn't have any truck with venture capitalists, he said, but he'd had a confidential approach from the French construction giant Vinci a few months earlier and we could pursue that. We did, and in February 2008, a few months before the crash, we sold our shares to Vinci plc for almost £8 million. Buying Gordon Durham & Co obviously gave the French a taste for British building companies, as Vinci's other main purchase that year was Taylor Woodrow Construction.

When I left the others to negotiate the details of the sale and went home alone to the flat I'd been living in since the breakdown of my 20-year marriage, it seemed like time to take stock of my life. I felt I'd achieved one important part of my destiny, in terms of developing the skills needed to create this wealth and realise it, while taking care of my own wellbeing. Yet my life, as a whole, still seemed far from balanced.

I had achieved something significant and achieved the financial independence I wanted. But there are other things in life.

It wasn't until three years later, in 2011, when I was relaxing on holiday with my new wife, that I began to feel I'd achieved the equilibrium I'd been seeking – the balance of wealth and wellbeing, of really being me, that I now know as WealthBeing. I'd got there the hard way, almost by accident, without ever really knowing what the end goal was or what I needed to do to reach it. I wasn't even sure exactly where it was that I'd arrived. All I knew was that it felt great and it was a good, calm, positive place to be. This book is about helping you to get there, too.

WealthBeing and you

So is WealthBeing for you? If you feel frustrated and dissatisfied with being an incomist – living off an income, or, to put it more harshly, being a wage slave – or you've already made the move out of the corporate world but are still not properly satisfied, maybe it is. Did you realise long ago that you had had enough of dealing with the pressures of being an employee, that constant sequence of challenges from above, over which you have little or no control, and for which the reward is so often just to be given yet another challenge? If this is the kind of thing that leaves you blocked and demotivated, then WealthBeing may be what you need.

Rather than continuing as an employee, looking to others to judge your capabilities and achievements, it can give you an opportunity to apply your talents in a way that will create wealth for you and improve your wellbeing.

And here we come to the first obstacle to overcome on the way to WealthBeing.

Can you do it?

It's natural to doubt yourself. It's also natural to leave this key question unanswered. In fact, it's so natural that some people leave it unanswered for a whole lifetime or at least until it's far too late.

On the other hand, if you listen to some coaches and teachers, you'll hear them say that we can be whoever and whatever we want to be. That is equally unbelievable to many of us. We all have plenty of experience of success and failure, but nothing that necessarily tells us that we can do anything we set our minds to, without any regard to the limits of our capabilities.

So who is right? What is the reality? Is it your own self-doubt or the gung-ho optimism of the coaches and teachers?

In my opinion, it is neither. It seems to me that, for any given role, there are some skills and attributes which make a person more or less likely to succeed. They may be natural or they may be learned. But, one way or another, you need to either have them or acquire them if you are going to succeed. You may not want to acquire them, or you may feel unable to acquire them. Most people tend to believe that they can't do what they see others doing well, because they make it look so easy and must therefore be blessed with some god-given talent. But Matthew Syed, in his excellent book, *Bounce: The Myth of Talent and the Power of Practice*, shows that it is purposeful practice, rather than any innate skill, that makes the vital difference between failure and success.

> For any given role, there are some skills and attributes which make a person more or less likely to succeed

The truth is that you can work towards WealthBeing as long as you possess, or are willing to acquire, just three key attributes:

1. You know how to win.

2. You want things to be better.

3. You are prepared to play the long game.

These are the three essentials you need to create WealthBeing. You can't do it without them. But the good news is that they are also *all* you need. Let's look at each of them in turn.

Knowing how to win

Creating a business demands that you get resources (customer contracts, employees, supplies, money and so on) from others, which you do by beating the competition for those resources. There are two subtle but important differences between knowing how to win (and then going on to do it) and the requirements of corporate life, in which the aim is usually being (or being seen to be) the best.

1. Feels better, because you get to choose where to compete.

In corporate roles, you are usually grappling with tasks set by your superior and your performance is judged against others to see who, in the opinion of the boss, is the best. You can change jobs, or even change career path, but you can't escape the pressure to play other people's games. In running a business, you're in charge. There's no requirement to be the best at a task set by a superior. Instead, it's about winning the game that's currently being played, such as the 'game' of securing a sales contract. On the corporate ladder, you signed up to being given tasks by others. When you're running the show, you get to decide which games you play. Successful generals

> Successful generals are the ones who choose their battles carefully

are the ones who choose their battles carefully, and this is the same principle. You choose the battles, thereby increasing your chances of winning. And winning battles of your own choosing, with the resources you can bring to bear, is a lot less stressful and more satisfying than competing to do something you have no real desire to do.

2. Feels tougher, because you have to find the resources.

In corporate life, every task or role comes with access to resources – a budget, people at Head Office, consultants or suppliers whose skills you can draw on. When you are creating something yourself, you need to find the resources to make things happen – and they're not always in the obvious places. You'll have to forge links between people and things that were previously unconnected. You may have to take two steps to get what you need. You do this by asking for the resource and then listening carefully to what people say. Sometimes the answers are clear, but often they're opaque, with other names to contact or odd reasons why it can't be done (which, in themselves, may give you clues as to how to solve the problem).

I was once able to help my business partner, Richard Brooks, by making just this sort of unexpected connection. Richard was the chairman of an innovative supermarket, a social enterprise with its customers as members, which was struggling to stay afloat. On the day we were meeting in London, someone had suggested I should also meet Paul Barry-Walsh, a self-effacing entrepreneur whose charity, the Fredericks Foundation, helps support worthy enterprises by providing loans when the banks have said no. As soon as I met Paul, I saw the potential for putting them in touch with each other. I told him of the supermarket's fight for survival and brought the two men together. They clicked, the pieces fell into place and an outline deal was agreed in less than an hour.

Look at your daily life and see what evidence you can find that this is you:

- ▸ The outcome of small, everyday battles can indicate that you know how to win. Do you somehow get a seat on the train? Do you get your round in quickly, even in crowded bars, without elbowing others aside or causing offence? Do you win at cards, Scrabble or golf more often than your talent would justify?

- ▸ Everyday problem situations can reveal how good you are at finding and utilising resources. If someone is taken ill on the train, do you wonder what to do or are you the one who makes the call and asks someone to alert the guard? If a hire car breaks down in the middle of a foreign country, do you get it fixed and find a way to get back to the resort or would you rely on your partner do it?

Wanting things to be better

Sometimes the ways of the world get us down. As children, we spend a lot of time learning how it all works. As we go through adolescence, we question things until we realise that it really can be 'so unfair'. We generally adapt to this reality by avoiding situations we don't like, spending as much time as possible doing things we like and putting up with the rest, accepting that we are individually unable to change it.

Sometimes we experience problems or repeated situations we want to get away from, but can't, unless we change something. We get tired of cutting ourselves shaving and finally get round to buying a different razor. At other times, we can't find a solution that makes us happy and we resolve to create one. King Gillette was so fed up with the honing, stropping and accidents associated with cut-throat razors that he invented the first proper safety razor. Colonel Schick hated all that foam and water and invented the electric shaver.

Sometimes this feeling is less specific. It's not attributable to a particular problem, but a general feeling of dissatisfaction that won't go away.

We are broadly content with what we have but there's something missing, in us and in the world around us. I don't know what drives this – our restless curiosity, perhaps – but I do know that it happens to many people. And when it's sufficiently acute, that's when it's time to think about changing your working life and considering WealthBeing as one of the options that's open to you.

When you recognise this feeling and acknowledge it, you are nurturing your independent thinking, which is essential if you are to develop something that didn't exist before, and so, hopefully, make things better. Some people say this is what lies at the root of the hero's quest that was first set out in the ancient myths and legends of Greek and Latin literature.

Playing the long game

Heroes like Odysseus had a tough time of it, battling monsters, sirens, cannibals, whirlpools and shipwrecks at every turn. One of their distinguishing traits was that they never gave up, and eventually they succeeded.

You may say that in today's ever more materialistic world, we don't need to put up with such suffering – or any suffering at all, for that matter. Instant gratification is the order of the day, and online access to support, advice and assistance can resolve almost any issue. If that's what you think, you may well be right. But since these actions and reactions are quick and easy, they don't affect us deeply. They don't

> Working towards something that makes things better, and achieving it, fulfils deeper needs than those we satisfy in our daily living

provide us with deep feelings of wellbeing. It is my contention that a sense of wellbeing comes not from a series of short-term highs, but from something more powerful: the knowledge that your life has a bigger purpose. Working towards something that makes things better, and achieving it, fulfils deeper needs than those we satisfy in our daily living.

Abraham H Maslow, a pioneering American psychologist of the 1940s, developed this line of thought by defining a Hierarchy of Needs, which he said motivated and drove every human being. According to Maslow, we are only truly fulfilled when we have met them all. There are several versions of Maslow's Hierarchy of Needs, but the one I am using distinguishes eight levels of need:

1. **Physiological** – food, sleep, health, sex.

2. **Safety** – health, home, security.

3. **Love** – including family and social connections.

4. **Esteem** – the need for achievement and independence.

5. **Cognition** – a search for knowledge and meaning (and, yes, that does include the meaning of life).

6. **Aesthetic needs** – finding beauty, truth and goodness.

7. **Self-actualisation** – realising all your potential, being free from superficial concerns and internally honest.

8. **Transcendence** – guiding others towards achieving self-actualisation.

I expect you will have met the first three levels of needs to a substantial degree. The desire to make things better is part of the need for esteem. I hope to show you how to achieve that, and also to help you fulfil the higher needs. For example, creating a new business, an idea that improves some people's lives, is one way of giving life meaning. The environment that you will create – the culture of the business and its relationship with the outside world – should contain beauty, truth and goodness, while the wealth you will have will free you from superficial concerns, as well as being one way of showing that you have realised your potential. Having achieved that, you will then be able to help and guide others (as I am trying to do here).

The needs listed by Maslow are not so very different from those recognised by the exponents of NLP (neuro-linguistic programming). NLP teaches that we have six essential needs, which can be mapped quite closely to the needs listed in Maslow's Hierarchy of Needs.

NLP	MASLOW
No direct match	Physiological
Safety	Safety
Connectedness to others	Love, including social connections
Uniqueness	Esteem (independence)
Individual growth/change	Esteem (achievement)
Meaningful contribution	Cognition
Freedom of choice	Self-actualisation
No direct match	Transcendence
No direct match	Aesthetic needs

This is a slightly rough and ready comparison. You might argue for a different mapping, with 'meaningful contribution', for example, seen as being more like 'self-actualisation' or 'esteem'. But precise mapping is not that important. The key point is that both models make a pretty good stab at encapsulating the basic human needs of people living in 21st century society.

NLP theory reflects the belief that each of us ranks those needs slightly differently, whereas Maslow's thesis is that we all need all of these things and rank them in the same order. This apparent clash can be reconciled if we accept that Person A's need for cognition, for instance, may be more easily met than Person B's. For example, Person A may feel that being a parent fully satisfies his or her need for cognition, while Person B may need to get back to work in order to satisfy this need and may be prepared to accept a reduced connection to others (in this case, the children) to achieve this. People know what they need and they make their own trade-offs to suit their personalities.

Being practical, I suggest that your own sense of wellbeing will be deeper and more long lasting if you know you have done the right thing, rather than if you just did whatever made you happy in that moment. Asking your staff to work late on a Friday (it's always Friday!) to get an important job or proposal done may produce short-term unhappiness. But it helps to generate wellbeing in the long term. Even if the proposal is rejected by the customer, you will know that your choice was the right one for yourself and those you affect, because it moves you onwards towards your greater goal. The sense of being determined to do the right thing is powerfully self-sustaining: it feels good to do it and so you do it consistently. Recognising this is important, as this knowledge is a tool you can access when you are facing another unpopular decision, and it will help to ensure you maintain a robust sense of wellbeing.

Some basic tools

Creating something new is rewarding, but challenging too. Doing things differently is always more risky than doing what you know is safe because you've done it before. I want to help you feel able to deal with this risk and manage your feelings and actions. The best general approach is to look at the alternatives at each stage and find a way through. But some things are applicable to every stage, so let's equip you with those now.

Good information Using this guide and the other resources mentioned in this book will take away a lot of the risk factors, because you will have a much better chance of making the right decisions. And where a decision is not clear, don't make it. Put it off till later. This is not the world of the stock market, where fund managers and traders face the urgent imperative to make decisions now because they are being judged against the clock.

In 2012, I climbed Mt Kilimanjaro. It's over 19,000 ft high and a colleague of mine, an ex-captain of the Welsh rugby team, once described it as the toughest challenge he'd ever tackled. I wasn't the first up there. I wasn't even the first in my group. But I made it – and there's not all that many of us who have ever looked down across the heart of Africa from its snow-capped peak.

It's the same with WealthBeing. It's not a race against time, nor against other people. Achieving it is a personal challenge you set yourself. But when you get there, it will give you a good feeling that will last you the rest of your life.

Good feeling You can only meet your need to create something, well, if you feel good. And to really feel good, rather than climb a mountain every day, you need to check in with yourself and find out if you do. This means finding yourself some head space, learning to relax and probably learning the art of meditation. Meditating is commonly associated with spiritual or religious activity, but there are some wonderfully easy and effective meditation techniques that are not spiritual at all. They simply help you to relax, stop being driven by your thought processes and gain an ability to observe your thoughts and feelings. All you need is a quiet space and a simple step-by-step mindfulness tool, such as Headspace. There's a link to it on my www.wealthbeing.co.uk website.

Give it a try for 15 or 20 minutes a day for three weeks. You'll be amazed at the difference it makes to your life. By the third week, you will be able to feel more in control of your feelings, even in bustling public places, just by changing your breathing and concentrating on being present. This is the primary skill that Headspace teaches. Once you have the ability to go inside yourself like this, you can take a look around, see what your body is telling you, discover what your mind is thinking about how you really feel and start to hear what your inner, unquenchable spirit is saying to you.

Negative information When things aren't going well, we sometimes see the next steps leading inexorably to catastrophe. When we're talking about situations and problems that are new to us, this risk is all the greater. But catastrophes are actually extremely rare, and can only usually occur in an unlikely set of circumstances. In fact, it can be surprisingly helpful and reassuring to look into the abyss and examine the chain of circumstances that would need to occur for your situation to turn into a catastrophe. It's like looking over the edge of a cliff. You peer over with your heart filled with dread, expecting a bottomless drop. But that's the first surprise: you can see the bottom. OK, it's a long way down, but it's not infinite. Once you've turned it from infinite to finite, you've taken the dread away. You've empowered yourself to examine the situation, to begin to understand it clearly and then to start looking around for the resources you'll need to help you resolve it.

Negative feelings Sometimes you do this kind of thing emotionally, too. Your emotions create a vicious circle, and you're unable to see a way out. In this case, you need to take a close, forensic look at your feelings and see if you can spot the apparently logical step that takes you from 'Here is a problem' to 'I can't solve this problem because…'. Then examine your reasoning and see if it's really true.

> It's always hard to see exactly where
> you are when you're in a hole

The fact is, it's always hard to see exactly where you are when you're in a hole. You need to get a broader perspective. Discussing the situation with a trusted friend or adviser may help, but I would also recommend learning to apply modern mindfulness techniques, which can be very useful in coming to terms with negative feelings.

Moral commitment A recent survey, set out in the book *Moral Courage*, by R M Kidder, found that good people in cultures around the world share a surprisingly consistent commitment to seven moral principles:

1. Honesty, integrity and truth.

2. Responsibility and promise-keeping.

3. Respect, equality and abiding by the law.

4. Fairness and impartiality.

5. Compassion and tolerance.

6. Love.

7. Freedom.

It's obvious that some business people don't stick to these principles. But creating and growing a business – even a large and successful one – does not require you to breach these moral rules. There will always be the minority who allow the urge to win every time to overcome the desire to do the right thing. Kidder's theory is that the minority is missing out and that learning to adhere to the proper principles – to do the right thing, even when it may be difficult or dangerous – is a rite of passage to maturity, fulfilling a basic human need that is not unlike the Maslow Hierarchy's need for esteem.

No-one can be sure they will do the right thing until they're tempted. And temptation came for my father in the mid-60s, when he was offered lucrative building contracts by a well-connected Northern architect, John Poulson, on a private and unusually non-competitive basis. Dad refused his advances and Poulson was later gaoled for seven years for bribery and corruption, bringing down with him the Home Secretary, Reginald Maudling, and dozens of senior civil servants and council leaders. As a result of my father's scruples, the company's reserves were a lot lower than they might have been when faced with the industrial strife of the 1970s. In the disastrous winter of 1979, when barely a brick was laid, the firm was on the brink of insolvency. But the business had retained its integrity, and a few loyal clients, and it was eventually able to trade through the tough times and go on to further success.

Openness to unexpected solutions You may not know where or what the solution is, but if you stay open to the possibility of a predictable miracle, it will often turn up. This phenomenon, known as synchronicity, was first observed by Carl Jung in the 1920s. As long as you stay true to your moral compass and committed to your path, things can happen – often quite out of the blue – that help you along it.

In 1979, when bankruptcy was looming and the country seemed to have come to a stop, Gordon Durham & Co suddenly won a major contract to build a large number of council houses for the Washington New Town local authority. This one contract kept the company going, provided work for hundreds of builders and tradesmen and generated enough profit to recover most of the previous year's losses.

Physical health There are many books and videos devoted to maintaining your physical health, so please forgive me if I devote just one paragraph to this important area. That is because I firmly believe that the only principle to observe in looking after your physical health is 'everything in moderation'. As you've probably noticed, one year's research findings are frequently stood on their head by the next year's study. Even water can be a health risk.

If you stay open to the possibility of a predictable miracle, it will often turn up

In 2003, during one particularly demanding theatrical production, Anthony Andrews, the BAFTA and Golden Globe-winning actor whose career has stretched from *Brideshead Revisited* in the 1980s to *The King's Speech* in 2010, forced himself to drink as much water as he could – up to eight litres a day. He collapsed, suffering from water intoxication (hyponatraemia), a near-fatal disturbance of brain function that results when the body's normal balance of salt and electrolytes is pushed beyond its safe limits. Andrews spent three days in intensive care before being declared out of danger.

Eat, drink, sleep and take exercise in moderation. And if you find that you have eaten or drunk too much, or failed to go for a walk for two weeks, be kind to yourself. Forgive yourself and get back on to the path.

So, if you feel you have the three characteristics you need – you know how to win, you want to make things better and you're prepared to play the long game – and that these tools have equipped you to manage any feelings of nervousness, then you are ready. I invite you to start on your journey into the future, towards WealthBeing.

Outline of WealthBeing

If you know how to win, are dissatisfied and feel that you want things to be better – and can see the benefits to yourself of aiming for a bigger, longer-term goal – you are entirely suited to the quest for WealthBeing.

At each stage of the process, we will look at how to achieve wealth – how to create a business, build it up and sell it, and how to have sufficient wealth to be free from superficial concerns.

At each stage we'll also make sure that you can look after your emotional wellbeing, understand the emotional challenges you will face and cope with the changes in your life.

The basic outline of WealthBeing looks like this …

Creating it

WEALTH

The starting point is creating a suitable product or service. This involves **bringing something new to what you know** – innovating in a market you're familiar with and **creating something you can be good at providing**, using your skills and experience.

We'll make sure you avoid picking a market that's full of powerful competitors or a product that's only in demand in the good times by choosing a product or service that solves a problem that is **common but not severe or uncommon but severe**.

We'll make sure that **it fits** – that it can be used today and doesn't depend on something else before it can be bought.

We'll make sure **it's priced properly**.

WELLBEING

You'll feel vulnerable, of course, but it's not necessary to be unthinkingly brave and 'feel the fear and do it anyway'. Instead, we'll show you how to look at the downside, to **stare into the abyss** and recognise one very reassuring truth – even if this venture fails, you'll still be better off.

You'll discover the art of **resourcing yourself**, so you can learn as you go, and **dealing with your dark side**, which is out to sabotage your plans and needs to be put firmly in its place.

You'll learn not to rely on parents, friends and life partners to make the big decisions for you. They care about you, but they have their own perspective on life. They will give you some support, but in essence **you are on your own. And that's exciting.**

Launching it

WEALTH

Then it's time to launch it. I shall help you to **spend less**, and to understand that the short-term sacrifice of a year or two without the luxuries you're used to will make the success you achieve feel even better.

I shall explain why you only need about **£50,000** to start and how to find that money.

I'll show you how to use friends and forums to identify customers, and how to make sure they **like and trust you**.

I'll help you find ways to **demonstrate benefits**, rather than features and explain why your product is faster, better or cheaper than the alternatives. If you don't get a buying signal, you must learn to move on to another target, even if this was supposedly 'the big one'.

WELLBEING

If you're confident you can make your new product or service, sell it and manage people – or you nearly can – the best plan is to get a mentor alongside you to top up your skills.

If, as is most likely, you are comfortable in only one or two of these roles, the answer is to **find a partner**, work with this person for a while without making a total commitment and then, if everything looks good, join forces properly.

If your product or service hasn't worked as well as you'd hoped, you must **re-engineer it** and see if there is a better product to be made or a different problem you can solve.

And if that doesn't work, you must congratulate yourself on having tried it and see if you'd like to start something different. Many of the world's most successful people **failed at least once before finding success.**

Nurturing it

WEALTH

You must make sure that what you're offering is **good** quality, not 'quite good', but not 'perfect', either. If you make mistakes, **say sorry** to your customers.

You must learn how to spread the word about your product or service with **case studies and stories**.

If you need distributors, you must make sure you're working with people who are **capable**, have the opportunity to deal with customers and are **willing** to do so.

Realistically, you must learn to manage your resources on the basis that **it will take much longer** than you thought to achieve a comfortable level of revenue.

When you get the opportunity to negotiate sales and purchase contracts, you will sell more and build more profitable relationships if you learn to **think win-win**.

WELLBEING

As your business grows, you will need to develop a culture and an infrastructure. The culture will shape the infrastructure and should **ensure that your people feel useful** and free to do whatever's best for each customer. The infrastructure should be flexible enough to let this happen.

To make sure that everyone gets this, and that it works, you and your people should make a commitment to sticking to the Three As – Agree, Accept, Amend – when arriving at decisions. When considering any proposal, people should either:

Agree with what's suggested, explicitly

Accept what's been put forward, despite any personal reservations

OR

Amend the original proposal.

Expanding it

WEALTH

It's important to recognise when you have momentum and **move quickly** to make the most of it.

Expand your sales by being visible, having **conversations** and building on what has already worked.

Create channels to market that will give you greater visibility, but make sure that you don't lose the ability to negotiate a win-win.

Acquire resources flexibly, paying a higher price per unit, if necessary, but spending less in total.

Keep an eye on the balance sheet so you don't run out of cash.

WELLBEING

Though working in the business can make you happy, you need to **work on the business** if you're going to be able to sell it. Becoming a leader in this way can enable you to satisfy several of your essential human needs – for esteem, self-actualisation and transcendence. If that isn't going to be the right role for you, recruit an MD to lead the business and find the right part for you to play within it.

You'll need to recruit and manage a team. **Hire for attitude and to enhance existing skills**, ensuring that the team has all the different talents and expertise it will need, and manage by reference to a vision and values to which everyone has contributed.

After growing or maintaining sales and margins, most of the problems in any young business will be to do with people's performance. **Have 'fierce conversations'** to resolve them. But if this fails, don't be afraid to let people go.

Look for win-win solutions to even the most upsetting issues. **Avoid a fight**, because you won't win, even if you win!

If you're stuck, ask yourself **10 questions and change everything.**

If you **get 70% right**, you're succeeding. If you're up to 80%, you're doing well. If you think you're getting 90% right, it just means you're not taking enough risks.

Building and selling it

WEALTH

As soon as your business has some substance, you should start planning for its sale. **It won't last forever** – and without a sale you won't have the financial independence that's an essential part of WealthBeing.

Set out a strategy that explains **its unique or nearly unique place in the world**, and demonstrate how it achieves its results, numerically, with **independent management and robust processes**.

Expand into **new markets or new products, but never both at once**. Don't rush to fund these externally – and, if you do, make sure that you really will be better off.

Calculate how much you need, by looking at comfortable living costs and listing those things that only happen for a certain period of time (such as education fees). This is not blind guesswork, and most people's needs are remarkably similar. As a result, your sums will almost certainly lead you to a figure in the £2 million to £5 million range. This is your target.

The value of the business will be between three and eight times its annual profits (in most cases, **4–6 times** profits). So you will need to generate profits in the £300,000 to £850,000 range.

WELLBEING

You must learn to look at the business as an **asset**, something to be bought and sold, rather than as the creator of your income.

Negotiating the sale can be intimidating but **don't be overawed**. The purchasers are just human beings like you, even if they have access to larger sums of money.

You must know when and **how to say no,** and how to make sure you leave **something for the purchaser**.

Making predictions about the rest of your life is a bit scary, but **using the calculation tool** I have provided will ensure that you have enough for your future needs.

Deepening and caring for your WealthBeing

WEALTH

When you have the money in your hand, invest it in **things you know about** or in shares and loans of publicly quoted companies (**stocks and bonds**).

Returns from stocks and bonds should be 2–7%, after costs and inflation and before tax, (with **3–5%** being the commonest range).

WELLBEING

While it's usually impossible to spot the right time to buy or sell stocks and bonds, you may feel better if you are able to identify a particular opportunity.

After the business is sold, things will come to a stop and **you may feel low for a while**. If that feeling stays with you for more than a few weeks, seek counselling or other help.

If it doesn't, you can start to enjoy your new state and consider the next journey. What is it that makes you **happy**? What is **meaningful** to you? It may be a new business, or it may involve **serving others**. Just being able to act without the limitation of needing a financial reward is an exciting and liberating sensation.

This journey will take you where you want to go, if you stay curious, ask questions whenever you can and see where the other person's answers may take you. If the answer is not what you expected, see if it works as well as – or better than – the one you had in mind. Then you can either ask another question or walk away.

For each step of the WealthBeing journey, I have included a financial picture of how the business might look at that stage. This is important, because business is easy until you put numbers to it. In Chapter 6, I will give you a practical approach to calculating how much wealth you need.

It's not so easy to measure WealthBeing at each stage, but this graph may help you to see how the total amount of your wealth and wellbeing might change along the way:

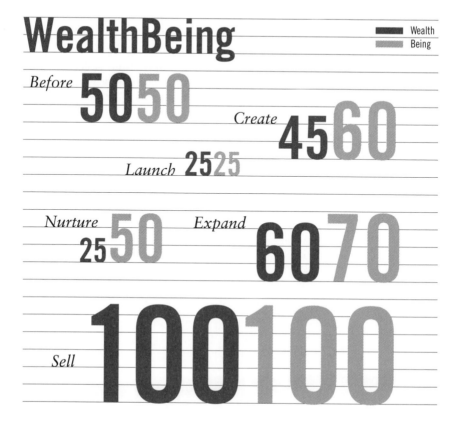

This book is a guide, not an instruction manual. All I am trying to do is provide you with the essence of each item so that you can create and implement your own plan.

We are all taught to think about complex problems so that we can come to decisions. But what we aren't all taught is that thoughts don't produce actions. Emotions do. Feeling strongly enough is what makes us get up and act to change our lives. So if you feel you could create WealthBeing for yourself, let's look at the practical ways you can do it.

Stay curious: ask questions
whenever you can

2 CREATING IT

Introduction

Let's start with the creation of your product or service. Ideas can come at you from all sorts of angles. Sometimes they are even given to you. The idea for my original business, FD Solutions, a flexible finance director service that allows companies to hire an FD by the hour or the day, rather than on a full-time employment contract, came from an FD I was meant to replace. He told me this way of working was the next big thing. So I mulled the idea over, evaluated it and decided that I could start doing it myself. My evaluation answered four questions:

1. What is the problem that I can solve?

2. Could I be good at providing this solution?

3. Does my solution fit?

4. Could I provide it at the right price?

Having answered those questions, I decided to move forward. But I needed to feel that it was the right thing to do before taking any action. So I looked at two further considerations:

5. Was I comfortable with and committed to the venture?

6. Did I have the necessary support of others?

This chapter will help you get the right answers to all six questions, ending up with a useful WealthBeing check.

A problem that you can solve

As people strive to achieve their own wealth and wellbeing goals, they face problems they either have to or would like to solve. The number of people facing each of these problems varies – some of them are common and some are rare. But it is important to understand that the type of problem you are solving determines the likelihood of your venture being successful. The greater the need to solve the problem and the more people suffering it, the bigger the potential opportunity will be.

This little matrix diagram illustrates the four possible mixes of severity and frequency of problems:

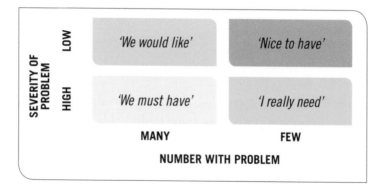

Solving a problem is most likely to bring you success if that problem fits the sky-blue boxes (top left box and bottom right) shown here, because these have enough customers and not too much competition. Let me show you what I mean.

1. You should avoid the light blue box (bottom left) because in big markets, with many people suffering a severe problem, there will be too much competition. Suppliers in these markets are usually big enough and ugly enough to beat you, even if their product is inferior or more expensive. They will shout louder than you (via advertising and PR) or simply squeeze you out by

matching your price for as long as it takes for you to run out of funds. Entry into this kind of market demands enough capital to spend on mass marketing to get your message heard, and on being able to stick around long enough to become profitable.

2. I've met may people who aim for the dark blue box (top right), where the market is made up of a small number of customers, who, they think, would love the luxury product they are planning to launch. In good times, when the economy is growing, this seems like a quick and easy way to earn a handsome profit. Occasionally it is. But the problem with selling to a few people who want something nice is that it will be the first thing they economise on when money gets tighter. It's also the hardest kind of product to provide, as people's requirements are very varied. If you think something's nice to have, like a handmade shirt, you may easily be persuaded, by your friends or by something you read or see on television or online, that the colour or cut should be different. If it's something that you must have, like a safety harness for your new windsurfer, the requirements are clearer and easier to meet. Upmarket designers and others who supply luxury products traditionally get round this problem by persuading their customers that the designer knows best, or by quietly cutting back on product quality and durability while retaining the look. In areas where this isn't possible, yachts and cars for example, there is a long list of famous businesses – Westerly Yachts and Aston Martin are two that spring to mind – which have failed to survive and whose original owners are long gone.

So the sky-blue boxes are the best places to be if you're trying to create a product that will generate WealthBeing. You need to find yourself an area where there are a few people with a severe problem or lots of people with a significant one. Providing finance directors to small and medium businesses on a part-time basis, as I originally did, generally meets a significant need of lots of people (though for a few the problem is severe). But it is not an issue that lots of people must have solved, nor is it something that only a few customers would like to see a solution to.

The usual advice you'll get at this stage of the thinking process is to do some market research. But this is only really likely to be useful for businesses in the light blue box (bottom left), working in large markets with lots of data. A better next step is to make sure that you understand your market. That is best achieved by having been in it, so you have a real, personal understanding of the nature of the problems and the kinds of solutions people want.

Your idea doesn't necessarily have to be something related to your professional area of expertise. It could be to do with a hobby, a sport or a particular personal enthusiasm. The important point is that you must know a lot about it.

On the other hand, you really don't need to know all the ins and outs about how you are going to create the business. We'll come on to that in Chapter 3, where I'll be giving you a fair bit of hard-won practical knowledge, gleaned from my own experiences and those of the companies I've watched and helped over the years.

Being good at providing it

As I mentioned in the introduction to the book, some problems irritate people to such an extent that they go off on their own and look for a solution. By dint of hard work, set off by a flash of inspiration, they invent the electric lightbulb or the bagless vacuum cleaner, even though they originally set out with no idea how to do it. If you, too, are determined to follow this path, just go ahead. I wish you every good fortune along the way. Ignorance is bliss. Not knowing enough about what you need to do can make you think it will work out in the end, just because you'll keep working at it until it does. It can happen. It did for Edison and for James Dyson. But the stats don't look good.

WealthBeing recommends a different path, with a far higher chance of success. For every triumphant James Dyson, there are hundreds of failures that are less well known. You don't read about them in the papers. But I've been an FD and adviser to many enterprises, and I have seen all too many of these heroic failures.

> For every triumphant James Dyson, there are
> hundreds of failures that are less well known

I have seen accountants set up as washing machine manufacturers and sausage makers start up restaurants. In each case, they failed because they didn't know what was needed. They just didn't have the experience of those markets.

I'm not immune to the lure of a big idea like this. I've been tempted too. When I was originally wondering what kind of business to launch, I initially ruled out the thing I was best at. At the time, I was the youngest finance director of a fully listed public company in Britain. But, as often happens when you find something relatively easy, I was a bit bored with it, and I'd managed to kid myself I could be anything I wanted to be. Software was (and still is) a large, rapidly growing market. So how about a new accounts package for small businesses? Or what about corporate finance? I had some experience of this, too, and could have set myself up in this field, where the money's good and the work can be more exciting.

But sanity prevailed, in the end, and I decided against these alternatives. My reasoning was simple:

- ▶ I was less experienced in these areas than I was at being a finance director.

- ▶ I knew many of the pitfalls of software development, but I didn't know how to get round them. Until I did, I would never be an expert in this field.

Contrast this reasoning with someone who came to see me recently. He'd been successful in managing large IT contracts, and his new plan was to set up a health business. My advice to him – as it would be to anyone planning a similar leap from their known to their unknown – was simple and blunt. Don't do it.

- ▸ If you have a brilliant idea for a market in which you have no experience, find someone in that market to license the product from you.

- ▸ If you understand a problem and what the solution is, find someone to create a workable solution and license it from this person or create a partnership.

- ▸ If you are still determined to go ahead, give yourself time – a lot of time – to learn about the market and what its experts know.

The other advantage of working in an area where you are an expert is that you understand what existing products can't do or what needs are completely unmet. One fertile area to consider is the impact of changes in the regulations that govern your specialist field.

I mentored a lovely little business that traditionally runs payrolls for tiny firms with one or two employees. When disabled people were first given the chance to spend their benefit money themselves, they found themselves employing their own carers. This new requirement wasn't something they could easily handle and my friend Diane spotted this and offered her help. Councils were grateful that she was around to iron out this wrinkle in the new system and a thriving new business came into being.

Diane hadn't been looking for a big idea. Even when she realised she could extend her services into this new area, it took a long time to recognise what a great opportunity she had stumbled on.

At the other extreme, if you are not well versed in the area you plan to operate in, it is quite easy to persuade yourself that your big idea is a worldbeater. And it's always worth asking one key question: 'If this is such a great innovation, why isn't someone in the industry already doing it?' There are bright people in most industries, and they may have spotted objections that you have missed.

'Ah, but what about the passion?' you may ask. 'I've been in catering for 20 years and I feel the urge to change direction and do something else.'

Well, that's just what you will be doing. You won't create a business of value, which will be worth several million pounds to a hardheaded buyer, if you are the only, or even the principal, executive. It would not be a business that was independent of you and that could be bought from you. It would be an organisation with you at the centre – and it would have no value without you. The passion you feel should be invested in the desire to create something significant, thereby satisfying some of the higher needs in Maslow's Hierarchy of Needs, rather than in doing more of what you've already done. Several of these higher needs may also be met by achieving non-financial goals, such as giving something to society, or to your own industry, by showing others how to execute well. Though I am only one of 20 FDs working in my business, and they all have masses of experience too, I still enjoy explaining to them about the finer points of finance or about the business we are running.

You may have noticed that I have deliberately avoided any hyperbole about being the best. Being the best is a false goal, and it's an ambition that has led many businesses into terrible trouble. There is no need to invest heavily in creating something perfect, way ahead of the competition, either at this stage or any other.

People with long memories will recall the fate of Boo.com. This much-hyped e-commerce site – a darling of investors and trendy commentators during the Millennium dot-com boom – went spectacularly bust after spending $135 million of venture capital money in 18 months, even though it was heavily promoted. Its software and technology, I am told, was a thing of rare beauty, having been bought in at a cost of $70 million. Only a handful of customers ever got to enjoy it, though, as Boo went from 'best' to 'bust' within six months of starting trading.

At the other end of the spectrum, entrepreneurs are often tempted to launch the business while the product is still 'in beta'. There's nothing wrong with launching something that doesn't yet have all the features it could have, as long as it has the features it claims to provide and they deliver the benefits that are required. You can sell a petrol-engine car now and bring out a diesel version later, as the petrol-powered vehicle is still a car. But a car that stops unexpectedly and won't go again until you've wound down the windows and flashed the headlights three times is not a car that will sell (though, of course, we all know the feeling – that's exactly what badly developed software feels like).

This good-but-not-perfection approach should help you avoid overspending on over-ambitious product development. That, in turn, will mean you have less money to recoup and take less time getting to your break-even point. Make sure, though, that you're not deceiving yourself about your product's capabilities. Use the Good Information and Good Feeling tools in this book to help you stand back and look clearly at it to ensure that it really does what it needs to do. And if it doesn't quite do that yet, just keep quietly working at it. As I said before, there's really nothing to be gained by rushing.

Does it fit?

A product people will buy has to fit into the chain of goods and services in which it sits. If the product requires other things to change before it can be used properly, it will take time to be accepted, if it ever is.

For example, it has been possible to download video content for many years, but it wasn't until broadband became readily available and easy to use that services such as the BBC iPlayer became popular. Some people identify this by saying 'it's a 2011 product'.

Sometimes the barriers are not so obvious. My own service was 'a 1999 service', which I created in 1991. The cost savings were clear for all to see, but managing directors worried that having a finance director who was not available full-time was too risky. 'What would happen if you weren't around when the bank phoned about a bounced cheque?' they'd ask me. So for eight years, until the internet became widely accepted, my product didn't fit. Once businesses went online, good communications and information management did not require colleagues to be in the same building all the time and the rules of the game changed. From 1999, we were able to clock up growth of 40% a year, time after time, until the recession hit us in 2009–10.

If you're not prepared to wait until the problem is fixed, you could try to fix it yourself. I would advise against this since it requires two sets of solutions: one for the problem you originally solved and the next one to allow people to access your product. Some of these access and infrastructure problems – such as charging points for electric cars – can only be solved by very big businesses. As an SME, you wouldn't be tempted to try setting up a nationwide network of charging points. But it's easy to fall into less obvious versions of this kind of trap when creating software, for example. If it doesn't load up simply and work alongside the other operating systems and applications your customers are using, it doesn't fit yet. And you won't be generating the sales you need until it does.

The right price

Pricing needs to take account of two factors:

1. The price of competing solutions, when comparing the total cost of each.

2. The profit you will make.

Competitive pricing

You may be selling a familiar, easily identifiable product, such as vodka. In this case, the price it can be sold at is determined by the price of vodkas generally, and the positioning of your vodka in that space – is it mid-range, luxury or a commodity? The market price is well established and you can slot into the appropriate segment, depending on how your negotiations with the customer go (which we shall look at in Chapter 3).

If you're selling a new solution, it will help enormously if you know – and, ideally, can quantify – its benefit to the customer.

In 1997, I was asked to help a company that sold tracking devices that enabled fleet owners to see what was happening to their vehicles. The tracker showed the fleet operator where vehicles were, where they were heading and how fast they were going. It was a good idea and it attracted £1 million of investment capital. But the company failed because it never managed to put a credible figure on the cash value of the service to its customers. Competitors who could provide this missing link made the sales instead and are now well-established businesses.

Even if you appear to be the only provider of this solution, remember that there are always other alternatives. Even if you have a patented product, this rule still applies.

I spent many years helping, and even investing in, the makers of a patented sign technology that could provide neon effects using screen-printing machinery. It was a great, eye-catching product that offered an affordable alternative to non-neon signage, though it was slightly more expensive. The new technology and the extra effects were impressive, but customers didn't feel they had to make the change. Not enough did and the company eventually folded.

You should also look at the basis of charging – per unit, per hour, or some other basis. The clearest example of this is in training. When I quote for giving one day's training, I could charge £1,500 and feel that this is a good hourly rate. But if I can negotiate per-head pricing and charge £500 per trainee for the day, I will make more as long as more than three people are involved. My clients will find it clearer, too, as they won't have to keep checking how many people are coming and whether the price has gone up or down.

Profitable pricing

Most of the guidelines I'm offering in this section apply equally to products and services. But profitable pricing means focusing on different considerations, depending on whether you are selling goods, services or software.

If you are selling goods, your costs will be made up of the cost of purchase from the supplier, manufacturing or modification costs, and overheads. You can identify material costs and component costs by getting estimates from potential suppliers and from your own industry knowledge. The more you know about your product, the more successful this exercise will be – because, of course, there isn't one market price for goods, except for consumer goods. Without a good knowledge of what you're buying and experience of dealing with these suppliers, you will not get a price that is low enough to make a profit. And even if you do have a feel for the market, your new product is likely to involve additional costs, which will remain unclear until it has been made in quantity for long enough to provide evidence of practical details. These details might include the time it takes to make and the amount lost in, say, evaporation. As long as these 'known unknowns' are no more than about 15% of the cost (which you or another expert in the process should be able to judge), the venture is reasonably assured. But do make sure you identify all the costs, and don't assume that just because something seems trivial it will be small.

I worked for a short while with a drinks manufacturer that had managed to negotiate fiercely competitive prices from the different subcontractors it used for all its production, bottling and packaging processes. Its problem was that it had to move the goods from one supplier to another after each stage. This seemingly trivial matter made a big difference, in the quantities the company was making, gnawing away at margins until the profits were wiped out and the business had to cease trading.

To get a useful costing for each product, it is necessary to add staff costs and overheads that relate to your manufacturing activity. This is best done by following the principles of Activity Based Costing (ABC).

The aim is to find out how each activity relates to the end product, identify the costs involved and then attribute these proportionally across the products. Here is an example, based on a factory where different work groups make different things. They all have similar work areas and use similar equipment, so we can allocate costs fairly simply, according to the number of people working on each product.

PRODUCT			A	B	C	TOTAL	
	Staff Salary & NI pp	£'000	15.0	16.0	17.0	n/a	
	No. of Staff	No.	4	5	3	12	
Direct Costs	Total Staff Salaries	£'000	60.0	80.0	51.0	191.0	
	Manager's Salary	£'000	25.0	30.0	35.0	90.0	
Attributable Costs	Premises Costs	£'000	10.0	12.5	7.5	30.0	Split in proportion to number of people
	IT Costs	£'000	4.0	5.0	3.0	12.0	
	Total Cost per Product	£'000	99.0	127.5	96.5	323.0	
	Marketing	£'000				10.0	
	Admin	£'000				15.0	
	Total costs	£'000				348.0	

It is not necessary to allocate all the costs to each product, because not every cost is driven by the amount of direct activity that is carried out. For example, directors' time is spent on building the company and managing quality, and allocating it would require the directors to measure how much time they spent on general business activity and how much they devoted to each product offering. Even if this could be done accurately, it's not useful because it's not determined by the volumes produced or the number of products, but by what needs to be done to develop the business, including maintaining product quality, which is not the same thing as manufacturing the product itself.

When it comes to services, people rarely bother to analyse costs properly. There is a tendency to assume that you can't allocate costs to each individual offering because you can't measure the costs of the people providing the service. In fact, though, you can.

In 1993, I was the finance director of a company that provided telephone support to sellers of computers and software. It had a telephone system that could manage calls – quite revolutionary at the time – with a module we had bought in that reported the time spent on each call. This allowed us to calculate the cost of calls by product. We allocated staff costs according to the time spent, added on premises and IT costs in proportion to staff numbers, and then used the results when calculating tender prices for new contracts. This information ensured that we were able to present highly competitive bids, even when the service was still new and largely untried. But we were also able to share the assumptions on which a bid was based with customers and incorporate them into our service level agreements. This meant that if we performed at the specified level we would not only make a profit but also keep our side of the bargain with each customer. This solid foundation enabled us to win business from leading software companies, get investment backing from 3i and sell the business for a good price two years later.

The challenge of understanding the cost of your product is particularly acute when it comes to software, where the unit cost to reproduce the item is only a few pence, but the cost of making the first one is many times the price you will sell it for.

To arrive at a realistic price, add together all the costs of developing the product. The main item here will be what you pay your developers, including their office costs, if they are employed by you.

This will give you a figure for the total cost of delivering each piece of software. To calculate the right price per unit, you will obviously have to divide this by the number of units you expect to sell. This can only be an educated guess, at this stage, because you cannot know how positively, or how quickly, the market will react. But your guesstimate will at least be informed by your experience. If you have followed my advice and created something that relates to what you know, you will be in a position to make a far better stab at this than anyone else could manage and you will be able to set your unit price at the right level.

The difference between the sales price and your direct costs is your gross profit. Having estimated costs and sales prices, you can calculate your gross profit percentage – the gross profit expressed as a percentage of the sale value. These percentages will differ according to the type of business you are creating and also to the efficiency with which you execute your plans. Comparing your gross profit percentage with those of similar businesses will provide a useful reality check. My website lists regularly updated margins for various WealthBeing-type businesses, but this table will give you some rough guidelines.

TYPE OF BUSINESS	DIRECT COSTS	GROSS PROFIT %
Software	Pressing CDs, Royalties, Sales Commission	80–90
Retail (including web sales)	Goods & Shipping	40–60
Branded Goods (including clothes, food, drinks, electronics)	Goods & Shipping	40–60
Manufacturing	Materials, Equipment, Power, Repairs	15–30
Distribution	Goods & Shipping	25–35
Professional Services	Salaries, Payroll Taxes, Pensions	30–40
Recruitment	Salaries, Payroll Taxes	25–40
Other Services	Salaries, Payroll Taxes, Pensions	20–35

The reason that competitors are similar to each other is that what one buys its competitors buy too. And because there is a free market for these goods and services, every buyer will pay roughly the same price. It is how many units are made and sold, and how efficiently this is done, that determines the profit each supplier will make. A difference of just 5–10%, well within the ranges I have shown in the table (above), is usually enough to persuade people to change suppliers.

You may be innovating by buying from a new source or changing the terms offered to suppliers, and this may generate margins that are higher than those generally seen in your market. If so, be realistic. Make sure that you can hold on to this advantage by agreeing contracts with at least two suppliers.

FD Solutions employs most of its staff, but its competitors generally use sub-contractors. This means FD Solutions has higher fixed costs than its rivals. Nevertheless the extra cost is not enough to seriously affect margins, and when an FD employee performs well, the bonus structure ensures that he or she is well rewarded. The salary element enables us to recruit higher-calibre people, which gives us a consistent competitive advantage.

Committing to the venture

So you have decided that you have the attributes necessary for WealthBeing (knowing how to win, wanting things to be better and being prepared to play the long game) and that you have a solution to a problem that fits, is priced at a level that works for both buyers and seller and can be provided by you, consistently and well. The question now is not whether you can do this but whether you will. An intelligent person can always think of a thousand reasons not to do something. As Kipling said 'We have forty million reasons for failure, but not a single excuse.'

There is a widespread belief that accepting a challenge, from others or from yourself, necessarily means being brave and ready to 'feel the fear and do it anyway'. A talented lawyer once said that I was brave to do what I was doing. But I never saw it that way myself. Instead, I went through a three-stage process, a version of the 'looking into the abyss' tool discussed earlier:

1. I understood that I was now 'consciously incompetent'.

2. I broke the enterprise down into its essential constituents, analysed them and saw that they were reasonable and achievable, in that I could become competent in each of them.

3. I looked at the downside and decided it wasn't too bad.

Consciously incompetent

There are four stages of learning anything. Take walking as an example. As babies, we are unaware that we can't walk, so we are unconsciously incompetent. Pretty soon we become aware that others are walking around and we aren't, so we are consciously incompetent. Then we start to walk, with great care and effort as we become consciously competent. Finally, when walking becomes second nature to us, we become unconsciously competent.

If looking at creating a business is something you haven't done before, you are not competent and you know it. That's the beginning of the learning process. With this book, your own, growing experience and the support of others, you will be able to acquire the competence you seek in this area.

If you try to launch a business in an area in which you are not already skilled, you will be unconsciously incompetent, not even knowing what you don't know.

Essential constituents

At the heart of every business is a simple equation. You gather people together who make or provide something for £x and sell it for £y. The difference between £x and £y is your gross profit. You sell enough so that the costs of employing and supporting the people are covered by the gross profits.

By reviewing your decisions so far you will be able to reassure yourself that this is the case. You know how much it costs to make your product (within a margin of

> The question now is not whether you can do this but whether you will.

15%), you know what price the market will bear (also within about 15%) and you know that there are plenty of people who have this problem, but not so many that it will attract too much competition.

Peter Dawe founded Pipex, the UK's first commercial internet service provider in 1988. When BT and others eventually woke up to the opportunities in this market, it became clear that it would be difficult for smaller companies like Pipex to prosper in a world of corporate giants. Dawe recognised that this part of the business landscape had changed for ever and sold the firm, going on to launch another 60 different companies.

BJCunningham created Death, a cigarette brand with the daringly counterintuitive marketing message that smoking is bad for you. But its trademark rights were challenged by an alcohol company called Black Death and the legal fees eventually forced it under.

Downside

What happens if the venture you're planning doesn't work? This isn't something that is widely discussed. People whose ventures have failed often try to hide the fact. But the reality is usually not as disastrous as it may seem. You'll probably have lost a year's income and whatever you have spent on the venture (we'll come to that later). But as long as you stop before the financial exposure becomes too great (which we shall address in Chapter 5), you won't lose your home. You may still have some savings and you are unlikely to be unemployable. The fact that you have been through this kind of tough learning experience marks you out as someone special, and companies are always on the lookout for special talent.

There is also the possibility that one of your new contacts will ask you to work with or for them, in ways you probably hadn't considered.

We all have a dark side, a tendency to sabotage ourselves. This was best demonstrated to me on a training course when I was asked to take a plain piece of paper and draw a line two-thirds of the way down. As we each started to draw the line, our teacher said 'Your dark side is telling you that that is not two-thirds of the way down.' I hesitated and started to doubt my judgement, even though I'd already worked out quite carefully where the two-thirds point would be. But the teacher was quite right. If you're trying to do something significant, your dark side is always going to be hard at work telling you that you can't. Recognise this, and tell it that you can.

If that fails, take a piece of paper and draw yourself a picture of your dark side. I don't know what yours looks like, but it will probably look rather ugly. Place it on a cushion, and hit it with a shoe (the original saboteurs were anti-automation protesters who threw sabots, or wooden clogs, into weaving machines to wreck them). Keep going until you feel that dark side is firmly put in its place. If it reappears later on, do it again. In the end, it is actually indestructible, but it can be made small and insignificant.

Finally, check in with yourself and see if you get a good feeling, the second tool that we discussed in the introduction to this book.

Your supporters' club

No man is an island, and you will undoubtedly want to share your idea with others. It's natural to feel sensitive about doing this. Musicians, for example, frequently mention the fear of rejection the first time they perform a song they've written, and the anxiety around launching a new venture is much the same. To deal with it, you must recognise that the perspectives of parents, friends and others around you are different from yours. When you acknowledge this, you will still be connected to them, but in a different way. You are going off to do something new and this necessarily distances you from them. Once they get the chance to see you in your new roles – and there will be several, as we shall see – they will be able to reconnect with you.

Parents

Parents want the best for their children. Having watched you fall over, literally and metaphorically, for many years, they may be filled with panic at the prospect of you apparently volunteering for another fall. The stock reaction is 'Why are you leaving such a good job?' or, if you have been made redundant, 'Why not get yourself a proper job?' These reactions are par for the course. Emotional support is a bonus, and any financial support is rare and valuable.

If your parents have sensible questions to ask, you should answer them and avoid becoming defensive. The inevitable question, 'Why would anyone buy this?', is one that's always worth asking. Making a real attempt to answer it clearly and analytically is a good test of your ability to manage your emotions and will usually earn you some parental support.

Life partner

It is reasonable to expect your life partner to be supportive, as long as you recognise the extent and limits of that support. He or she is committed to you and your wellbeing, as you are to him or her.

But there is no rule that requires your significant other to commit his or her personal wealth to the venture, too. It is often helpful if your partner has an income from elsewhere that can either provide for your entire needs, as a couple, or make a significant contribution to them.

Creating a business is like having a child. My business is as old as my son and the feelings I have towards them are similar. The difference is that your partner is unlikely to have quite the same feelings towards this 'stepchild'. If you have children, you may sometimes seem callous when you have to put the needs of the business before those of your own kids. Nativity plays and sports days, tender submissions and go-live dates don't make comfortable bedfellows. A frank discussion about this, recognising that there will inevitably be some clashes but that you may be free to provide care at other times, could help to ensure that each of you feels properly supported.

> Creating a business is like having a child... The difference is that your partner is unlikely to have quite the same feelings towards this 'stepchild'

Friends

Friends support each other. This feels good, but beware of being misled by casual remarks that may be badly ill-informed. When listening to friends' opinions about why someone would or wouldn't buy your product, try to gauge whether they are looking at it as customers, experts, informed critics or casual observers.

Your best friends are those who listen well and relate their comments to what they know, rather than what they feel. Don't rely on well-meaning advice that says 'I wouldn't do that – I'd do this', because that is your friend's choice, based on your friend's feelings, not yours. You'll get the most value out of listening to those who keep their emotions out of the conversation and have some relevant knowledge. They will help you see if you have truly demonstrated a complete chain of logic that leads to: 'Yes, this type of customer would buy it, because…'.

Comedians, who are always effectively launching a new product with each new joke or sketch, know all about this. A joke requires a coherent logical chain, too, if it is to be funny. In fact, the punchline is usually the insertion of the crucial last link in the logical chain. So it's a good idea for you to follow the process the stand-ups use when trying out new material. Their rule of thumb is simple: if three audiences don't like it, it's never going to work. If you find that three trusted friends don't follow your chain of logic through to a resounding 'Yes', there's something wrong and you need to find out what that is. It may be the product that's not right. But it may be something else. Perhaps, as discussed earlier, the product is ahead of its time and simply doesn't fit yet.

Everyone else

The reactions of everyone else are also worth mentioning, because everyone else – taken together – will add up to the market, or the economy. Don't get hypnotised by what the media pundits are saying about the state of the economy. You can start a successful business whether the economy's growing or shrinking, though there are different considerations to be borne in mind.

> ▸ In a growing economy, sales are the easy bit, but supply can be the problem. You may find you're short of staff or can't get essential supplies or services when you need them because, say, BT doesn't have enough engineers to connect your cable.

▸ In a receding economy, supplies are not the issue. The big risks are overpaying for them and not being able to charge enough for your product. Things people need are more resistant to economic downturns than things they want or would like. The more boring or essential the item is, the better sales are likely to hold up in a recession.

You can start a successful business whether the economy's growing or shrinking

WealthBeing check

Wealth

Your plans are taking shape. The market is out there, just waiting for you, and the time seems to be just right for what you have to offer.

Stop. Don't jump too soon.

It's not time to quit your current position yet. You should plan to leave that as late as possible. In the meantime, while the venture doesn't need all your time, fit it in around your existing commitments. A few late nights and busy weekends now may pay off handsomely later.

You may also need some money, at this stage – often about £10,000 or so, to build working prototypes and maybe do some test marketing. It's important not to ask others to help with funding at this point. I have come across far too many horror stories of people who've put up small amounts of money in the early days and come back later with outrageous claims. You don't want an early supporter thinking that chipping in a few thousand gives them ownership of your big idea or even a half share in the company.

A now-famous author, at her first big public book-signing, was surprised to be handed envelopes by several of her fans. Her agent, though, snatched them away and wouldn't let her touch them. The point was that these envelopes contained various suggestions and plot ideas the booklovers were putting forward. If the author had looked at them, it might have been possible for these fans to spot storylines in her later books and claim that the plot ideas were theirs, which could give rise to claims to a share of her very substantial royalties.

Your current financial position may look something like this:

	£'000
Your Salary	40.0
Income Tax on that	-10.0
Partner's Salary	25.0
Income Tax on that	-5.2
Total Income After Tax	**49.8**

	£'000
Mortgage Repayments	12.0
Child Care	5.0
Property Running Costs	5.0
Travel Costs	5.0
Food	10.0
Holidays	3.0
Hobbies/gym	1.5
Drink, Clothes, Entertainment	8.0
Total Expenditure	**49.5**

You should be able to find the initial funds you need for prototypes from your own savings, from family sources or even from a credit card offer. We will look at how you acquire further resources to create a business in Chapter 3, but at this stage the primary resource you need is a specification of the product and a cost sheet that shows costs and sale prices. This is your business plan. If you are creating a professional service, it may look something like this:

Professional Services Ltd – Business Plan
Assumptions (input cells in blue)

PEOPLE			CHARGEABLE				STAFF COSTS	
	Joining date	Hours (8/day)	%	Rate/hr	Value £'000	Salary	Bonus	
Self	Apr-15	900	50%	200	180	80		
New 1	May-15	900	50%	200	180	100		
New 2	Jun-15	1,080	60%	150	162	100		
New 3	Jul-16	1,260	70%	150	189	100	10	
New 4	Aug-17	1,260	70%	150	189	80	10	
New 5	Sep-17	1,260	70%	125	158	80	10	
New 6	Oct-17	1,260	70%	125	158	80	10	
New 7	Nov-17	1,260	70%	125	158	80	10	
New 8	Dec-17	1,260	70%	125	158	80	10	
New 9	Jan-19	1,260	70%	125	158	80	10	
New 10	Feb-19	1,260	70%	125	158	80	10	
New 11	Mar-19	1,260	70%	125	158	80	10	
New 12	Apr-19	1,260	70%	125	158	80	10	
New 13	May-19	1,260	70%	125	158	80	10	
New 14	Jun-19	1,260	70%	125	158	80	10	

NB Joining dates MUST be within plan period, not before

OVERHEADS

	Start	£'000	Varies	£'000	£'000	£'000	£'000	£'000
Rent	Apr-15	10	Per head	10	13	23	33	51
Admin	Apr-15	25	Per head	25	34	59	86	134
IT & Comms	Apr-15	12	Per head	12	16	28	41	64
Insurance	Apr-15	3	Per head	3	4	7	10	16
Marketing	Apr-15	20	30%	20	26	34	44	57
L&P	Apr-15	15	20%	15	18	22	26	31
		85		85	112	173	240	353

EXTRANEOUS

	%	No.
NI	13.8%	
Corporation Tax	20%	
Dividend Rate	50%	
Working Days (ex hols and bank hols)		225

Results

YEAR ENDING 31ST MARCH	2016	2017	2018	2019	2020
Heads (average)	2.8	3.8	6.5	9.5	14.8
P&L account	£'000	£'000	£'000	£'000	£'000
Turnover	480	664	1,126	1,609	2,436
Staff Costs	290	404	660	933	1,411
Gross Profit	190	260	466	676	1,025
Overheads	85	112	173	241	354
Profit Before Tax	105	148	293	434	670
Taxation	21	30	59	87	134
Profit After Tax	84	118	234	348	536
Dividends	42	59	117	174	268
Retained Profit	42	59	117	174	268
GP%	40%	39%	41%	42%	42%

I've listed employees who provide services at an hourly rate and are paid a salary and bonus. I've deducted overheads and Corporation Tax and paid a dividend to you and your other shareholders (we'll talk about them in Chapter 3).

But is this forecast right?

No, it never is. But it can be useful, without being right, just as long as it's realistic.

In getting to realistic numbers about your ambitious plans, I've found there's a sound rule of thumb: dream, then knock off two-fifths. I call it the Dream -40% method. When you're in the guesswork phase, with very little to go on, it produces results that are at least as helpful as any of the glib, misleadingly precise little formulae that you see bandied around by the supposed experts on small business.

I have also observed, from long experience, that growth is always likely to be exponential – it's hardly ever a straight diagonal line, climbing across the graph at a steady 45 degrees. Straight lines, based on the assumption that you will add so many extra sales each month, month after month, look pretty and reasonable, and they are easy to calculate. But that's about all they've got going for them. They don't reflect anything like the reality most start-up businesses experience. In real life, exponential growth is much more likely. Growth begins slowly, and is hardly noticeable at first. Then it starts to pick up and, all being well, it will suddenly begin to accelerate sharply. You reach a critical mass of customers, word starts to spread about your offering and all of a sudden there are a lot of people who have heard of it and are confident enough to buy it for the first time.

Sales by month/quarter/year

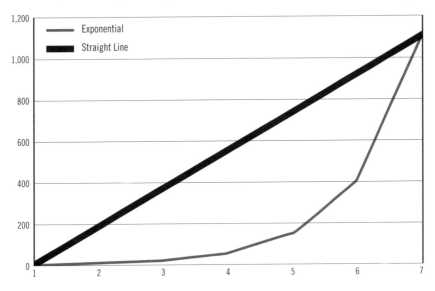

Once the business is up and running, you'll be able to make proper, informed forecasts – not least because you'll have real information coming in about contracts, buying cycles and so on. But when you're starting out and launching new products, the Dream -40% method can certainly serve you well.

Wellbeing

If you want to make a difference and you have an idea that appears to make this possible, you're already well on the way to achieving WealthBeing. But a bit of doubt and hesitation is normal. There is a good likelihood of success, if you follow my approach, but it's true that there are no guarantees. Still, the downside is limited – and if you succeed, you will be rewarded with wealth and a feeling of satisfaction and fulfilment that will sustain you ever after.

Hold on to this thought and take a minute or two to imagine what it will feel like to have succeeded, to have achieved something unique, started and driven by you. Read the rest of this book and reflect on how your personal journey could turn out. There will be obstacles along the way, of course. Everyone faces obstacles, and those that overcome them get there by finding the resources – and the people – they need to help them do it. You don't have to make it on your own to feel you have succeeded.

It may also help if you can bring yourself to see the next few years as a voyage of discovery – a huge opportunity to live and learn, rather than a chance to prove that you already knew what you had to do. Keep practising mindfulness. Whatever you do, I believe that this practice will improve your wellbeing. In relation to WealthBeing, it will help ensure that you can always look at your journey as a set of experiences to be enjoyed and learned from.

Success won't happen overnight, and it will be some time before you face the choice between continuing with the business or selling up. In my case, it took seven years to become established with an income that gave me a comfortable standard of living and a regular flow of work. I know that business plans rarely have a seven-year horizon (the one I showed on pp.63–64 envisages four or five years), but it almost always takes much longer than you think for ideas to catch on and spread. NESTA (a leading innovation think tank) has noted that many of the most successful businesses only grow significantly five years or so after they have been set up.

In my view, there is no need to feel a great surge of energy about the new venture. It's more a question of having a lightbulb moment. And there is certainly no need to consider yourself a worldbeater to achieve WealthBeing. Yes, you need to win sales. But you don't need to win every one. In fact, if you feel you do, you may be in danger of becoming obsessed – and that cuts both ways. Obsession can sometimes yield big gains

> You don't have to make it on your own to feel you have succeeded

in the area that you obsess about, but it won't produce WealthBeing. I am not a billionaire or a spiritual leader, but I am a millionaire and a leader. To be a billionaire or a world leader calls for complete single-mindedness and sacrifice, including the loss of things and experiences that you do want, but not as much as that one obsessive and overriding desire. WealthBeing is not like that. WealthBeing offers you a life that doesn't demand such sacrifices, but shows you a way to work towards the balance of wealth and wellbeing so many of us yearn for.

The net gain to your WealthBeing, around the time you set out on your new venture, might look something like this:

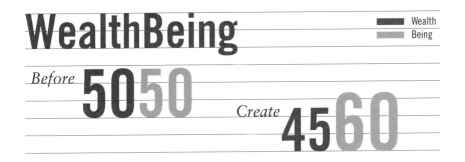

WealthBeing

■■ Wealth
■■ Being

Before 50 50   *Create* 45 60

Your wealth has been depleted a little, as the savings you had put aside for a rainy day have gone into the business. Yet already the creation of the new venture has given you a surge of wellbeing. If you keep on this path, good fortune ('where opportunity meets preparation') will soon follow. The money you've put in will soon be replaced by a steady and growing income stream and the building up of an asset you can eventually realise with a successful sale. On the wellbeing front, the new tools you have and the freedom and excitement of creating something new will give you the boost you need as you enter the toughest phase of the journey – preparing for the big launch.

3
LAUNCHING IT

Introduction

We have now got to the stage where you have a viable idea, which you are committed to. The next stage is launching it, and that will involve a sequence of four steps:

1. Making sure that you have enough wealth to survive, by spending less and raising some funds.

2. Making your first sales by promoting the product and closing deals on the right terms.

3. Looking at what needs to be done in terms of re-engineering the product, if it isn't working as well as you'd expected.

4. Ensuring that you have the necessary skills to create, nurture and expand the business, or that you know how to acquire them from a suitable partner or mentor.

This is the stage in the process when you are likely to feel most vulnerable, as you expose yourself and your idea, for the first time, to the harsh glare of commercial reality. But this is the challenge you have signed up to, and conquering it will give you the reward of a huge sense of achievement (one of Maslow's fundamental needs).

The result of following this process will be the creation of a viable business, one that is highly likely to succeed, though it won't start to show a profit for some time to come. You will also have created a team that provides all the skills and expertise you'll need, so that you can withstand any setbacks that occur and see them as nothing more than the next set of challenges to overcome.

At the end of the chapter, there is another WealthBeing check, to help you assess the progress you have made towards your ultimate goal.

Wealth to survive

The obvious thing to do at this point is to make a careful list of all the items you know you will need to spend money on, making cautious estimates about both sales (erring on the low side) and costs (pitching your estimates high), and do the sums to work out how much cash you will need. Within broad limits, this is fairly predictable. Even without knowing the details of your business idea, I can make an educated guess that you'll end up with a figure somewhere between £200,000 and £500,000. The idea of raising that kind of money is a daunting prospect, assuming you don't already have a track record as CEO of a substantial enterprise. You simply won't be able to do it, at this stage.

But that's OK. You won't have to.

All you actually need is enough to pay those people who won't or can't do you a favour by making, or helping you make, the prototypes and production models you need. As soon as you have these, you will be able to start showing them to prospective customers and distributors and making your first sales.

So there's no need yet to make significant commitments for costs like premises, equipment, advertising and PR. And it really is cheap to set up the legal and administrative framework for your new business. Buy a ready-made company (you can now do it online at Companies House for £15), open a bank account (you'll get a better deal if you go to one of the new 'challenger' banks) and that's it.

You won't usually need to worry, at this early stage, about health and safety and all the other regulations that may apply to your industry. Generally speaking, there are exemptions for very small companies. And even where there aren't, only the obvious regulations concerned with protecting the public are likely to matter. If you're serving food, you'll need to satisfy the health inspector. If you're selling financial services you'll need FSA registration. But that's about it. You can splash out on insurance if you like, but in my experience a common-sense approach to risk will get you through these first few months.

While the business will need funding of maybe £200,000 to £1 million over its lifetime, it doesn't need the cash now. In practice, the amount usually required is up to £50,000. This will be lower if the business idea is a service you can deliver yourself than if it is based on a product that needs to be manufactured. On the other hand, it may be higher, if you are developing a piece of software or opening a business that needs investments in premises, decor and equipment, such as a restaurant. Even then, though, it's good to ask yourself how far you could go with an amount that is 'gettable', in order to prove the concept and show people that it works. This would also enable you to show that you know how to use money well, which is always attractive to investors.

I haven't forgotten that you will still have to eat. You'll need to replace your income or reduce your expenditure until the business generates enough to start paying you. The more you need, the harder it is to raise it, so it's always better for you to reduce your expenditure and get as close as you can to living off your partner's income and your combined savings. If you don't have a partner, now is the time to go back to your college days and start remembering what it was like to live like a student.

A two-pronged approach will work best, so let's look at how you can:

- ▸ Spend a bit less.

- ▸ Get some funds.

> A common-sense approach to risk will get you through these first few months

Spending less

Look at the big items first. Think about how you can cancel, suspend or reduce your spending on:

- ▸ Cars.

- ▸ Health insurance.

- ▸ Contents insurance.

- ▸ Holidays.

- ▸ Gym and other club memberships.

- ▸ Pensions/savings schemes.

Check your utility bills, too, as they are probably taking more than they should. You'll use much less in summer than in winter, so make sure the estimated usage you are billed for is less than twice the winter bill.

Even if you do have a partner, it may help if you can think back to how you lived as a student. Remember those tricks like leaving your credit card at home and going shopping with cash. This will help you think more clearly about each purchase and can make a useful contribution to saving money.

It's also right to suspend your pension contributions and savings schemes, once you leave employment. Funds like this are designed to give you money for your retirement and will be superseded by the wealth you create by creating building and selling your business. When you get to the stage where the business is generating a profit and you haven't yet sold it, you can put some of this money into your pension scheme. Until then, you'll be better off focusing all your financial and emotional resources on one thing – the task of launching, nurturing and expanding the business.

These sacrifices may not sound like fun. But if you're determined to do something significant, they will feel meaningful, as steps towards your higher goal. It isn't for ever. And when it's over, the things you used to take for granted will seem like luxuries, and be all the more enjoyable for that. As the business gains momentum and starts to thrive, they may be superseded on your wish list by those things that emerge as being really important to you.

Funding

Until you have started to make things happen and you're able to show something that others can objectively view and assess (a seedling looks much more interesting than a seed), you're likely to be scratching around for cash. In the early days, the only people who will put up money to back your idea are you and those friends and family members who, firstly, believe in you and, secondly, are in a position to hand over the cash without being seriously hurt if they don't get it back. So the usual sources of funds at this stage are your own savings or redundancy money, and grandparents or parents who may be prepared to advance you a small portion of your inheritance.

That said, there are now a lot more places to find seed funding than ever before. The UK government-backed Start Up Loan scheme can advance £10,000 (or even, in exceptional circumstances, up to £25,000). You can borrow money from payday loan or similar companies, but this is an expensive route, with high interest charges, and one you should try to avoid. A better idea would be to make full use of all the credit cards you acquired

> A seedling looks much more interesting than a seed

when you were in employment. Crowdfunding is another possibility. Seedrs and Crowdcube are currently the leading providers of online marketplaces where you can pitch for the funds required to get you going, but the sector is growing all the time and the UK Crowdfunding Association now has more than 40 member companies. There are up-to-date links on the website for several of these firms and the industry is now regulated by the Financial Conduct Authority, so it is fast becoming an established part of the start-up investment scene. Statistically, the chances of successfully raising the funds you need are currently about 1 in 5, but it's worth remembering that some of the propositions will be a lot less well thought-out than yours and your odds should be rather better than that. If you have a product or service that appeals to consumers, you can offer discounts and sweeteners to those subscribing for shares who invest, say, £1,000 each. The charges for these services vary, but they generally come to 5% to 10% of the amount raised.

The next avenue is business angels, who nowadays are usually found in networks. Whereas the other sources of funds will not get involved in the development of the business, angels are different. They usually invest because they want to get involved and have skills to offer, as well as cash. If there is a good match between the skills that are on offer and the expertise you need, this could work well for you.

It's not obvious how to conclude a deal with an investor at this stage. The business is apparently worth nothing, because it hasn't traded yet, so what is it worth? What sort of price tag will investors put on a business that offers nothing but potential?

The pragmatic answer is generally between £100,000 and £1 million. That's a wide range, I know, but there are no hard facts to support anything else, just a few suppositions about costs, sales, pricing, volumes and market size. Investors at this level will accept this sort of valuation, even though they know that most of the horses they back will fall at the first fence, because they reckon one in every 10 of the companies they invest in will prosper and eventually be worth several million. Combined with the tax breaks, which usually reduce the cost of their investments by 30% to 50% and remove all capital gains tax exposure, this will potentially provide a good return on a broad portfolio of investments. In order to get to the higher end of these valuations, you should take potential investors through a simple calculation that shows how today's investment will translate into the appropriate share in the future value of the company. This example shows how an investment of £50,000 justifies a 4.1% shareholding:

Value of the company in 5 years' time	£3,000,000	A	
Investment required now	£50,000	B	
Required return on investment	30%pa	C	
Required value of investment in 5 years' time (increase by 30% a year or 150% in total)	£125,000	D	= B+(B*(5*C))
Value of investment in 5 years' time as a % of the value of the company at that time	4.1%	D/A	

Once you've presented this calculation, there will still be plenty of room for negotiation. The return on investment of 150% over five years (or 30% per annum – oddly enough, investors rarely seem to get hung up on the difference between simple and compound interest) that I have proposed is less than the 500% to 1,000% some investors seek when putting money into start-ups.

Some, but not all. Returns like that are possible, but they are rare. The problem for those pursuing the WealthBeing route is that you can often be tempted to put numbers together that will point to this kind of spectacular payback. Fiddling with your spreadsheets could easily make your business look like a much bigger and more obviously exciting prospect. But these huge payoffs are really very unusual. Even Facebook didn't start out like that – the social network was originally conceived as nothing more than a way for Mark Zuckerberg and his pals to meet more girls at Harvard.

Predictions that seem to promise the earth are easily disproved or disparaged, so it's better to stick to something that looks feasible and expect your investors to accept a realistic rate of return. After all, 30% a year, before tax breaks, is still a lot, and it's commensurate with the risk. If only two businesses in ten like this are going to make it (the rate will be better than the usual one in ten, simply because the results you're predicting are realistic and so this business is less risky than others) and the rest go bust, the after-tax return for investors will still be a generous 10% to 14%.

Stick to something that looks feasible

The other source that people often turn to is banks. While it's easy to find *offers* of £25,000 to start a business, it's hard to secure these loans and virtually impossible to raise more than that at this stage. This isn't a result of the Great Recession: it's always been so. At this stage, the bankers will see this primarily as a personal loan, so it needs personal security (in the absence of government-backed schemes) and the bank needs to be confident you have the ability to repay. A loan of up to £5,000 won't need tangible security, but above that the bank will look to put a charge on a suitable asset, which may be your house. Adding £25,000 to your mortgage is a common solution. The bankers will judge your ability to pay on their assessment of your business plan and their knowledge of you, so it will be helpful if you've been a customer for a couple of years. Needless to say, a plan that follows the guidelines in this book should satisfy them.

The last option is to get on with it, start trading and build up some capital with which to create a business of value.

> S ir Reo Stakis came to Scotland from Cyprus as a 14-year-old and made his first few pounds knocking on doors and selling lace handkerchiefs his mother had made. By the time he was in his mid-twenties, he had raised enough to open a restaurant, laying the foundations for a business empire, Stakis Hotels, which he eventually sold to the Hilton Group for £1.2 billion.

There are plenty of other inspiring rags-to-riches stories that follow this path, but it does take a long time to accumulate enough to invest in the new business and it's easy to be kept so busy looking after the trade that you never get around to launching the new venture.

One way or another, it is likely that you will assemble the funds you need from several sources. It's a good idea to separate out the money that is earmarked for the business and the cash you need to live on. This will give you an element of control and will also help your life partner to feel more comfortable, since she or he can then see a clear boundary between the two.

First sales

Everything we have covered so far has been about preparation, getting you and the product ready to be sold.

Now it's time for the acid test. Is what you have created something that is actually desired by people you have never met? This is one of the key questions that made you pause when you were considering your commitment, and you will have answered 'Probably, under some circumstances.' The very wording recognises the possibility of failure, of course, and acknowledges that people may reject your product and, by implication, you. This can be a paralysing thought, stopping us in our tracks and preventing us from doing things because we are scared of failure and rejection. But it's important to keep a sense of perspective here. Rejection of the thing we are selling is not a rejection of us. It's just a signal that what you are selling isn't what the potential customers need, or that the customers can't recognise that it's what they need. It's not a rejection of you as a person, and you shouldn't let it get to you in that way. If you are practising mindfulness, as I recommended in my introduction, you will be more able to manage this. You will notice if you are linking rejection of the product to rejection of you, and be able to conclude, more positively, that this isn't appropriate. This isn't rejection of you. It's just a difference of opinion, and that's OK.

Once you have broken that instinctive link between rejection of the product and rejection of yourself, you will feel happier about pursuing your first sales. This is a crucial stage in the launch of the business, and there are three things to address:

1. Promotion – finding your customers.

2. Engaging with customers.

3. Closing the sale.

> Rejection of the thing we are selling is not a rejection of us

Promotion – finding your customers

If you are selling to businesses ('business to business' or 'B2B'), your first task will be to find the right contact point, the right person to speak to in each company. If you and your business partner/mentor don't know the people involved, you should try to find someone, who one of you knows, who also knows your potential customer. If potential customers know your friend or colleague, that will validate you in their eyes (as long as the colleague has a good reputation, of course) and a meeting will follow. This is effectively what LinkedIn has done online, and it has become the basis of a huge worldwide business. As the social networking specialists have recognised since the 1920s, we are all connected to each other by no more than 'six degrees of separation'. There is some complex theory behind this, based on the mathematics of networks, but I see it in fairly simple terms. Each of us has an average of 40 friends and colleagues and 40 is 8 billion, which is greater than the world's population. Without pushing the theory to its limits, this means that you can usually contact someone in two or three steps, just by asking to be introduced by one or more of the people in between.

We all feel the need to play it safe and exercise some caution when coming across new things and new people, though, so one recommendation may not be enough. I have had more success when I am linked to someone via two (unrelated) connections. I call this the 'triangulation' process. It provides powerful reassurance if you can say: 'John, who I used to work for, introduced us, but I see that you know Bob, too. I was at school with him.'

If you are selling to consumers ('B2C'), the obvious place to find customers is the internet. It's possible that a well written website, with search engine optimisation and a tempting launch offer, could generate some sales for you.

Possible, but, frankly, unlikely.

The internet is a big place and 'pushing' your product at customers through the medium of the internet, without 'pulling' it, by pointing people to it, is unlikely to produce anything more than the odd random download. To find your potential customers, you must look for forums, Facebook groups, LinkedIn groups or chatrooms where people are discussing the sort of thing that's relevant to your product. There will be plenty. On a cursory trawl around the blogosphere, testing the limits of this assertion, I quickly managed to find:

  ▸   Over a million search results for 'gasket user groups'.

  ▸   Two million results for an impassioned campaign in favour of a return to old-style tungsten lightbulbs.

  ▸   A favourite album, with music I last heard 30 years ago.

Once you have found where the relevant conversations are happening, you can start to engage with the participants and invite them to your website, where you will have an opportunity to get their email addresses, and maybe some other information, by offering free downloads in return. Then you can send out emails to keep them interested and maybe to share with others. If they have given their email addresses, you should get past their spam filters, but you still have to persuade them to open your email. Do this by making sure your subject line fits at least one of four categories (the '4 Ts'):

1. Technical – it tells them 'how to'.

2. Tips – it has some 'top tips'.

3. Teaser – it's intriguing.

4. Take care – it's got a warning (that will be taken seriously).

Get their feedback on your product offering, put the positive comments up on your website and engage these people in conversation as much as possible. Apart from possibly becoming customers, they may have suggestions for improvements to your product or service.

Engaging with customers

Now you can make your pitch. Whether in person or on the website, there are only two things you should be focusing on:

1. You – because people buy from people they like and trust.

2. The benefits of the product – why it's faster, better or cheaper than the alternatives, with no hidden costs or practical obstacles.

The best definition of trust I know is set out mathematically in *Coaching and Feedback for Performance*, by Duke Corporate Education. It sums it up in a neat formula, equating Trust to the sum of Credibility, Reliability and Intimacy, divided by Self-orientation.

Whether face to face or on a website, you need to establish credibility – based on your experience of delivering this or similar products – and show your reliability, by referring to other successful outcomes. Until you've built up a track record and collected some testimonials, this is not easy to do.

But it's not impossible.

You do have a track record, and you can make the most of it by telling the world what you've done on LinkedIn, Facebook, Twitter and other emerging sites. People can check what you say and see for themselves who else you are linked to. Though the internet is a new way of communicating, we humans haven't evolved *that* much in the last 20 years. Most people still believe that you can judge a man by the company he keeps, so give them evidence of the people and businesses you've worked with in the past.

Intimacy, the feeling that you can be trusted to fulfil your promises, self-orientation, the degree to which you focus on yourself, and liking are all emotional, rather than analytical, qualities. So it's not what you do, but the way that you do it that gets results. If you are meeting a potential buyer, you can help to establish that you have something in common if you notice an award certificate on the wall or the car the person drives and make some appropriate comment. 'Nice car – I'd like one like that one day' doesn't start to build this kind of bridge between you. 'I drive a 4x4 too – they're much safer, aren't they?' does. The sort of language you use can influence the reaction, too. People who study NLP (neuro-linguistic programming) soon learn that each of us has a distinct preference for one particular sense channel when we are absorbing information. Some people prefer visual information, some pay more attention to the words they are hearing, and others need to touch and feel things before they take a new idea on board. You can often tell which sense people prefer by the sort of words they use themselves (expressions like 'I see' for visually oriented people or 'I hear you' for listeners). But you can also tell a lot by watching how they move their eyes. We don't look each other in the eye very often, and when we do, we look away. The direction of a person's glance when he or she looks away is a surprisingly reliable indicator of that person's preferred sense channel – up for eyes, across for ears and downwards for touch.

It takes a while to gauge people's responses. You may get neutral, or even negative, reactions at first – and this may be the way the whole conversation will go. But I would urge you to keep on trying until a connection is established. Without that, it is highly likely that your pitch is doomed. Again, mindfulness and meditation will help you to stick to the task. The practise of concentrating on one thing and one thing only (being mindful of it) actually gives you the paradoxical ability to do two

... mindfulness and meditation will help you stick to the task

things at once. In this case, it will help you keep up the conversation with the potential buyer while another part of your brain gets to work on analysing the responses you're seeing and working out the other person's preferred sense channel.

At some stage, you will be invited to get to the point. There is only one point to make – that your product is a **faster, better or cheaper solution** than any of the alternatives. To do this you need to understand the person's problem or concerns and relate the benefits of your product precisely to them. That means asking open questions, questions that leave the way open for a reply that's more than a yes or no answer. Open questions give you a way of asking what the problem is without suggesting an answer. Only when you have a shared understanding of this should you make your move and explain the benefits of your product. Again, it's important to resist the urge to tell people the solution. Just keep asking questions, but more specific ones, gradually moving from open questions to closed ones, until you get the yes you need.

This approach is more successful, because it acknowledges the customer's own point of view, and it's not that difficult. My own sales technique, if it can be called that, is to begin by asking 'Would you like to tell me about your business?' People like to be heard, so they are usually quick to share problems with someone who shows an interest. As I listen to what they are saying, I try to nudge the conversation in the appropriate direction, until it eventually becomes clear to all that the company needs certain things done, which, of course, can best be performed by getting in a part-time Finance Director.

> My colleague once spent 45 minutes listening to a business owner share her woes. His most significant contributions were 'Aha', 'Mmmm' and 'I see'. Her final comment was 'That was really helpful Stephen; when can you start?'

You'll notice that I haven't suggested you start by explaining the product. The fact is, no-one is interested, initially, in a demonstration of how your product works, because it's not their problem. Do you know – or care – how Facebook works, or your phone, or your washing machine? Your creation is there to solve a certain kind of problem. It's only when the buyer has agreed with you what the problem is, and how it might be solved, that you are on the path to proving your credibility, which can then be amplified by a demonstration or explanation.

Keep these short, too, or you'll lose your winning position. Start with your well-practised 'elevator pitch', a single sentence that expresses in a nutshell exactly what you do and why it helps. My standard elevator pitch for FD Solutions is just 14 words: 'We provide finance directors on an hourly rate who create positive cashflow for enterprises.'

If your product really needs a detailed explanation, limit yourself to ten slides with three brief points per slide. No-one wants to see any more than that. Each slide should be short and sharp, expanding on the opening statement and using both words and pictures so as to engage people with either visual- or aural-channel preferences. People can't read a slide and listen to you properly at the same time – and which do you think is likely to be more persuasive? Don't list the product's features without explaining their benefits, and don't include *any* unnecessary information. You can fill in the gaps later.

I recall asking a salesman once to show me why his software would match our statement of requirements, which had been sent to him in advance. He said he would, but my heart sank as he started his slide show with a detailed history of his company and its achievements. I can't remember now whether he said anything that was interesting or relevant, as I had glazed over before we'd got to the potentially relevant slides.

Finally, once you have successfully established credibility, reliability and intimacy, it's time for a bit of self-orientation – or, to put it more bluntly, to close the sale.

Closing the sale

Before you try to close the sale, check that you have answered all the customer's questions. Once that's done, you need three more things:

1. A buying signal.

2. An agreed price.

3. Some terms and conditions ('Ts & Cs').

With ready-made products, the buying signal will be an order, if you are lucky, or maybe a promise to come back (to the premises or the website). With more complex products and sales to businesses, it is rare for potential customers to say yes immediately. It's also rare for them to say no, directly, so you need to understand what is a buying signal and what isn't. A buying signal is an agreement to move on to the next stage of the process – for example to talk with superiors, to request a quote – accompanied by a deadline. Ask an open question, but this time make it specific – 'Who else needs to sign off on this?' – and listen carefully to the response. Typically, the answer you get will be either vague and defensive or specific and enthusiastic:

- ▸ 'I'll discuss it with the director' (Which director? And when?).

- ▸ 'I'll discuss it with Alan, my manager, at our new products meeting in June' (It may be a while away, but it's still a date).

In the first case you are unlikely to hear from this person again. In the second, you are implicitly being given the green light to get in touch on 1st July and ask how the meeting went.

You may say 'Ah yes, but this is a big customer, so they're bound to be cautious. I wouldn't expect a yes at this meeting.' No. That's not true. Big customers are more cautious than smaller ones, but they need to grow their businesses, too. If they can see that your product could help them do that, they will do something about it. If they can't, they won't.

You may say 'Well, maybe that person isn't the right person to speak to. If I got to the senior manager, I'm sure we could make the sale.' Again, no. The company has set this system up, making the salesman jump through the hoops and talk first to a more junior manager, precisely so that the decision-maker is not overwhelmed.

Does this mean that you have just one chance with your main customer? Probably. And if that fails, what should you do? Try somewhere else.

Einstein used to say that the definition of insanity was to repeat the same actions, while expecting a different result. You may have identified XX plc as the ideal customer for you. But if the people at XX are not prepared to take it any further, don't keep going back to them. Use your resources of time, energy and money to look elsewhere – and keep on looking until you get a buying signal.

This is what people mean when they refer to picking the low-hanging fruit. XX plc may seem perfect for you, but its fruit is currently out of your reach. The people there may change their minds eventually, but something will have to happen to make that shift occur. A change of personnel may indicate a slight possibility of this, but a more likely reason for a change of heart is the fact that your product is seen to be doing a good job elsewhere, leading the XX managers to reassess the situation.

The next key issue is price. Clearly, there is no sale without a price. When creating your product, you will have worked out what price would be both competitive and profitable, within a margin of error of about 20%. This is a big range and the difference is probably the difference between making a good profit and making none at all. When agreeing prices, there are five key factors to bear in mind:

> Einstein used to say that the definition of insanity was to repeat the same actions, while expecting a different result

1. There is an emotional element in every decision, and the fact that you have created something new won't, in itself, be attractive to many people. Human beings are creatures of habit. When you are making your first sales, the price advantage your product offers needs to be so attractive that it cannot be ignored.

2. Once your product is established, you can go on to charge higher prices that are in line with, or even higher than, your original estimate.

3. If you are selling bespoke items, you can raise your prices over time, on a case by case basis.

4. If your product is fairly standard, make sure the price you want to achieve is clearly visible, as a headline. To clinch your first sales, offer discounts, give stuff away or add in extras so your customers feel they are getting a bargain.

5. Your overall aim is to build up the business to a size where it has value and can be sold for a good price. Repeat business is always a powerful element in making a business attractive. So make sure that your post-launch pricing settles down at a level that works for your buyers and for you.

Finally, you need to consider the terms and conditions of the sale. As with insurance, just deal with the major items. You need to make sure that what you're selling is safe – it's a legal requirement to tell consumers of any risks involved (my favourites are McDonalds' apple pie, which cautions that the 'filling is hot', and Sainsbury's cashews, which are sold in a packet that says 'May contain nuts.') But where the other terms of sale are concerned, you can all too easily get pushed from the need to provide undertakings that the product is better than the competition to making promises you can't be sure of keeping.

Buyers understand that there is no such thing as a cast-iron 100% guarantee. A plane will fall out of the sky if the pilot makes an error and instruments malfunction in the middle of a storm – remember Air France's flight from Rio which crashed in the Atlantic in June 2009? This tragic and highly unlikely chain of events could not have been reasonably predicted and it didn't stop the airline continuing to make (implicit) guarantees as to its safety.

You do not need to issue over-generous guarantees to reassure your buyers. You should recognise that a query about guarantee terms will often be a slightly idle question, lobbed into the conversation as the potential buyer tries to see what the limits of this great new thing are. After all, what does a lifetime guarantee actually mean? I'm not particularly swayed by it, and I don't feel it's necessary for, say, a thermos flask or a mobile phone. I wouldn't want to be using the same phone in ten years' time. Instead, I recommend offering a clear statement of what the product's performance is expected to be,

> You do not need to issue over-generous guarantees to reassure your buyers

with a simple undertaking that you will fix it if it goes wrong. That's all most customers will need. Your main aim is happy customers, so if they're happy with that, you should be, too.

A business partner or mentor

Clint Eastwood, as Detective Harry Callahan, famously said, 'A man's got to know his limitations.' Dirty Harry wasn't specifically talking about setting up a new business, but he might as well have been. Creating a business demands any number of different skills, and it is highly unlikely that you will have all of them. In fact, there are three main skill sets needed to launch a business – sales, technical and management. You could look at these as 'outside skills', 'inside skills' and 'the glue to hold them together'.

We all have some degree of skill in each area. You may have got to this stage – of creating something, organising production or doing it yourself, and selling it – without a partner. But in order to progress, the company needs to be good at all these things.

> There are three main skill sets needed to launch a business

Not perfect, and not quite good.

Good.

Good is the standard that beats the competition often enough and minimises the issues with production, processes and staff we will deal with in Chapters 4 and 5. There are three ways to make sure that you can be good:

1. Be good, yourself, in all the areas that are important. This is rare and unlikely.

2. Find a business partner with the skills you are low on.

3. Find a mentor to help you develop the skills you are low on.

People who are good in all the requisite areas are probably not reading this book, or any other book for that matter! So you are likely to be faced with the choice between a partner and a mentor. A partner will reduce your risk, because he or she is always around to provide the necessary skills, and also, on the face of it, lower your return, because your partner will want a share of the value of the business (the equity). Mentors come with higher risks, because they are not always around and will often only advise, rather than execute. But the return will appear to be higher, because a mentor will take only a small part of the equity, or none at all.

Percentages of equity often interfere with our decision-making processes. As soon as we think of our ownership being anything less than 100%, we tend to see the business as a cake, with other shareholders taking slices of it away from us. It may take a real effort of will to persuade yourself, but this isn't what's happening. What the other person's involvement is doing is making the whole cake bigger. To make sure you make the right decision for you, keep thinking about the bigger cake and ask yourself two specific questions:

1. Can you acquire the skills you lack?

2. Will a mentor provide the emotional support that you need?

In assessing your own skills, the best thing to do is to examine what you do all day and divide it between external, internal and glue skills. Talking and emailing people with new ideas goes in the external (selling) box. Working on stuff goes in the internal (technical) box. Getting people to do things goes in the glue (management) box. See how much time you really spend on each area, and how long you *feel* you spend on each area – did the time fly, or did it seem to drag? Look at which things you do first, and what you put off doing. If you spend roughly equal amounts of time in each area and none of it feels like a chore, a mentor will do. If there is one type of stuff that you put off indefinitely and that

> Percentages of equity often interfere with our decision-making processes

seems to take a lot of time, I suggest you get a partner in. It will improve your chances of success and make you happier, too. And if you're happier you'll also be more effective. I enjoy selling and developing products, but when it comes to getting things done, I usually think a short email to the next person down the line is enough. It isn't, so I don't manage my business any more. That improves my net effectiveness, and certainly comes as a relief to those who had to suffer my management.

In addition to looking at complementary skill sets, you should ask yourself how you will make this experience a happy one. Even if you are one of the reasonably capable all-rounders who could learn and acquire skills from a mentor, and you get plenty of support from your life partner, you may still feel lonely in the business because there is no-one to share the journey alongside you.

Whichever approach you choose, though, there is still a problem. How are you going to find the right person to work with you on this engrossing and challenging project?

Partner

You can find partners in many places. Look among your business colleagues, on LinkedIn (there is at least one group specifically there to help you find partners) and on business start-up and trade association websites. Just mention what you're doing and what you need and soon enough people will start to put themselves forward for consideration.

As I said, people work best with those they like and trust, so apply the same rules when selecting a possible partner. You are looking for a match. This means that the partner should be as skilled as you are, in his or her own area, and have the same goal of creating something of value and eventually selling it. You may not get the 'finished article' this way – a high-earning salesman with a glittering CV, for example, would probably fit in better as an employee. What you will get is someone who shares your commitment and so will enhance both your wellbeing and your wealth. It can be lonely at the top. Having someone to share the problems with who has a different way of looking at them is the best way of avoiding this and making progress.

> People work best with those they like and trust

But you can't be sure of someone until you have seen how you get on and work together, so don't be hasty. Start with simple employment contracts, where you each take minimal salaries – enough for essential living costs, rather than the full commercial 'rate for the job' – and an agreement to share profits and equity after about 12 months. After the first three months, you will probably have a good idea of whether you make a good team. Assuming you have provided the start-up capital until the partnership is firmly established, you will retain the casting vote. So if things are not going to work between you, both parties can walk away easily – not too much older, nor poorer, and probably slightly wiser.

It is, of course, possible that the two of you will fall out at a later stage, raising the question of how to facilitate a parting that both find equally (un)acceptable. Whether or not it's written into a formal agreement, the likeliest steps to resolve this kind of dispute are:

- ▸ A sum of money, say £50,000 to £100,000, if the profits are still low, to reflect effort and salary foregone.

- ▸ If there are profits, a payment for shares which values the company at four or five times its annual pre-tax profits (this will become clearer in Chapter 6).

- ▸ A guarantee that, if the company is sold within 12 months of departure, your ex-partner will receive what he or she would have got if the partnership had continued up to the time of the sale.

It may not always be possible to make these payments at the time you go your separate ways (in which case, they can be made a liability that will eventually be settled out of dividends or via a buyout of the shares involved), but this is the kind of framework that can be used to facilitate an amicable and final resolution.

Mentor

It is often said that those who can do, and those who can't teach. Mentoring is fashionable now and has certainly attracted quite a few of those who can't, so you do need to be a little wary. You are looking for someone who has been, or maybe still is, a business person and who ideally knows your customers and suppliers. Your mentor does not necessarily need to have been in your industry, but knowledge of the customers and suppliers you will be dealing with will be a huge help to you.

Given the choice between a mentor who wants paying and one who is offering to put in time for free, I would advocate paying. If mentors don't place a value on their advice, it's probably not very valuable. If they do, it's likely to be worth having. Payment can be in shares, rather than cash, and the mentor may eventually offer to invest some money, too.

You may wonder why I haven't suggested the option of teaming up with both a partner *and* a mentor. To me, that's like having three people in a marriage. It may feel great to the person who has access to both, but the partner and mentor are each likely to feel that you are not fully engaged with them, as you share the views of one with the other. A better solution is to appoint a chairman or non-executive director who deals with both of you, openly and clearly.

Re-engineering

Whatever you have learnt and done, however carefully you have prepared, and regardless of your commitment, you may be unable to capture more than a handful of sales. Gradually, if you can let your analytical side have its say, you will come to the realisation that your new product is not going to work. There could be several reasons for this:

▸ Potential customers have declined to buy, at any price.

▸ You can't get it made and delivered at the price that will eventually make a profit.

▸ The product doesn't work as you expected.

If this happens, see if the product can be re-engineered to create a new product or a solution to a different problem:

▸ There may be a better way of solving the problem you originally identified, perhaps something you discovered while working on the first solution.

> ▸ Analyse the features of the product you have and try to see how they might be applied to other problems, maybe with one or two alterations. I know that this is exactly the reverse of the usual way of innovating, where you look at problems rather than solutions, but it's amazing what sometimes appears. The Dyson Air Multiplier, a revolutionary bladeless fan, was not created from scratch but by redirecting the airflow of Dyson's hand drier. The low-tack Post-it® note was invented by accident when 3M's technicians found their new glue simply wasn't strong enough to hold notes firmly and permanently in place.

It's also possible that the product doesn't work due to it not fitting. For example, your software is actually needed in remote locations, but those locations don't yet have the bandwidth to make it work. In a case like this, you may not need to do any re-engineering. Your best bet might be to mothball the business, just keeping it ticking over on a care and maintenance basis, and wait patiently until the market catches up.

Sometimes it turns out that events beyond your control change the situation and render your product obsolete.

The UK government-subsidised PV Solar Scheme originally paid homeowners 43.3p per kw/h for the electricity generated by fitting solar panels on their roofs. This generous feed-in tariff attracted many homeowners and many small solar panel installation companies sprang up to meet the demand. But the scheme was working too well, and the government wanted to put the brakes on. In March 2012, it slashed the feed-in tariff to 21p per kw/h, stretching the probable payback time for an investment in roof panels from about ten years to twenty. Demand evaporated overnight, householders didn't want solar panels any more and hundreds of installation companies went bankrupt in a matter of weeks.

Even if the idea was yours, and you took all the development and other decisions, you shouldn't blame yourself and consider yourself a failure. Many well-known business people have failed at their first attempt and been spectacularly successful the second or third time round.

Alex Chesterman is famous now as a serial entrepreneur, co-founder of Lovefilm and chairman of Zoopla. But before that he and his father set up Bagelmania, a chain of nine bagel bars, which could not keep pace with rising rents in central London and was eventually wound up (despite my assistance!). Looking at Alex's subsequent triumphs, I would guess that he learnt a lot at Bagelmania – maybe some of it from me.

In any event, you should congratulate yourself for having had the courage to try, and congratulate yourself again for having the determination to try again. Then, when the time is right, if you wish, go back and start again from the beginning, with something else. After all, you originally took on the challenge of launching a new venture partly because you were determined to make a difference. Maslow tells us that this need for achievement is one of our fundamental needs, and by starting down the path of creating something new, you have acknowledged that this is true for you. So be true to yourself and try again. There's no law against it, and you may draw strength from those people who admire your determination. They may even back you this time.

Samuel Beckett, the author of *Waiting for Godot*, summed up this philosophy of unsinkability in an obscure late-period novella called *Worstward Ho*. 'Ever tried. Ever failed,' he wrote. 'No matter. Try again. Fail again. Fail better.'

Fail better. Now there's a thought to keep you going through the dark days. If you are staying mindful, the ability to see what others call failure as just part of the human condition will be that much easier.

WealthBeing check

Wealth

I have looked through the accounts of more growing businesses than I care to remember. While they all have different levels of revenues and direct costs, depending on the industry and sector they are in, their gross profits tend to be strikingly similar, and their overheads also have many common features. Whatever your industry, the first stage of development is likely to take six to 24 months and look something like this:

PROFIT AND LOSS ACCOUNTS

Activity	Item	£'000	Comments
Trading	Sales	50.0	
	Cost of Sales	-40.0	Includes freebies, demos etc
Gross profit		**10.0**	**Margins will be low while getting established, unless you provide the service yourself**
Marketing	Travel & Subsistence	-8.0	You will have to go to them
	Website	-5.0	This can include online trading facility
Premises	Office	-5.0	You need to meet outside the home
IT/Comms	Laptop & Software	-4.0	
	Phones & Internet	-3.0	Being connected is vital
Admin	Bookkeeping	-1.0	You need to know the finances
	Sundries	-2.5	
Profit/(loss)		**-18.5**	

The state of the business at the end of this period will look something like this:

BALANCE SHEETS

Item	£'000	Comments
Fixed Assets	.0	**Don't capitalise your own costs, nor small items of equipment**
Due from Customers - 'Debtors'	5.0	**Make sure you get paid in 30 days or so**
Owed to Suppliers - 'Creditors'	-3.0	**You can get credit from the taxman but not much from other suppliers**
Working Capital	2.0	This is the net amount of debtors who owe you and creditors whom you owe. It will become important
Cash at Bank	28.1	**With a personal guarantee, you may be able to get a £25,000 overdraft**
Loan From You	-48.5	You'll need to pay the overheads and, say, half your cost of sales before the revenue arises
Net assets	**-18.4**	

You will have put £50,000 into the business. As sales start to materialise, you'll eventually have some cash in the bank.

Wellbeing

This doesn't convey the uncertain, hand-to-mouth existence that creating your business entails, as you try to avoid spending while waiting for the first sales that will prove your concept. The length of time it takes is down to luck, which is, as they say, 'where opportunity meets preparation'. The search for customers and the creation of the product will eventually come together, and suddenly – hey presto – you'll realise that you have turned your idea into reality.

Getting here is always the hardest part of the journey. Your WealthBeing graph may look something like this:

Your desire to do something significant has started producing some solid evidence. That will start to feel really good, though it will be tempered by the knowledge that there's still some way to go. You'll be tempted to reward yourself at this point by repaying some of your loan to the company. But it's best to resist this temptation, leaving yourself with more resources to create the significant enterprise that is your ultimate aim. Maintaining a feeling of wellbeing is important, though, and you deserve a celebratory treat of some sort. Reward yourself with an experience of luxury – a track day driving racing cars, a spa day with treatments and massage or a long, slow dinner at an amazing top-drawer restaurant. The reasons for rewarding yourself this way are quite important:

1. You will *feel* your success, rather than just seeing it in financial terms.

2. It's a one-off, so you won't increase your recurring costs. Counterintuitively perhaps, a luxury splurge will work out cheaper than many seemingly sensible bits of expenditure.

4
NURTURING IT

Introduction

So, starting with a small amount of capital, you have succeeded in creating a product, getting a partner or mentor, making some sales – and using up most of your cash.

The normal expectation is that the business will start growing now. But I'd like to add in an intermediate step, which involves nurturing the enterprise so that it has a stable, comfortable level of sales of hundreds of thousands of pounds, before the expansion that will lift it up into the millions. This will mean laying down the foundations that will enable the business to operate smoothly at this intermediate level. In some ways, these foundations are similar to the elements required when you were launching the product. They are:

a. Expanding sales by providing a good-quality product and spreading the word about it.

b. Managing resources, not just money, but time and people too.

c. Learning how to negotiate and say no, safely, to things you don't want to take on.

d. Accommodating your first employees, and establishing culture and infrastructure.

Again, we'll end this section with a WealthBeing check. I will show you the state of a business where orders come in fairly regularly, at a level where you can make enough profit to start paying yourself, and suggest how your WealthBeing looks. You'll know it's working, but others won't see it yet.

Expanding sales

Once a business has some sales, it starts to feel exciting, thrilling even. You're getting some tangible validation of your efforts. Before long, someone caught up in the euphoria will be heard to say that it's about to go viral or reach its tipping point. But you're not there yet, and you may never get there. These are rarefied places and not necessary for those aiming to achieve WealthBeing. There are three ways to expand sales now:

1. Offering **good quality**, which customers will tell their friends and colleagues about.

2. Finding more people to buy, by **spreading the word**.

3. Finding people to **distribute** your product.

'Good' may seem a vague word, but to me it distils and sums up exactly the quality standard you are aiming for.

Not quite good, and not perfect. Good.

Occasional excellence is OK, but it's not something that's attainable every time. 'Quite good' is not going to be enough to cut it. You need 'good' to make your business work.

When the reaction is summed up by this single word, without qualification, it means the emotional response to what you are doing is enough for people to want to tell others.

Good quality

While sales volumes are still low, you've got two aspects of product quality to focus on:

1. Getting it just right – big or small improvements.

2. Fixing it when it goes wrong.

Your first sales will be informal – friends of friends, a buyer who 'gets it', your old boss and so on. If they want changes made, it is imperative not to be difficult and not to get hung up on whether they are willing to pay for those changes. What they are doing is more valuable to you than that. They are giving you the benefit of their experience and their judgement, and what they say will help you to make the product or service good.

> You need 'good' to make your business work

They may be perfectly happy with it, at least the first few times, when they, too, are learning what it can do. Or they may have reservations or suggestions and be shy about telling you. Don't be shy about asking them. If you ask them, it shows you are interested in them, and that will make them all the keener to help you.

There may be implied promises. If they say 'I thought it came with blue ribbon', then send them blue ribbon. They may have got it wrong, in your eyes, but they don't think so. They have taken the leap of faith that's needed to get your product out there, and if they are happy, they will spread the word, at no cost to you. So just make them happy.

It's not that people never make mistakes. We all do. The important thing is that we are judged not by the mistake, but by how we react to it. If you have got something wrong, pay attention to it, say sorry quickly and clearly, and sort it out. If you argue, you will only produce resistance and aggression from the customer. You can see the dynamics of this if you put the palm of your hand in the air and flat against someone else's palm. What happens if you push? The other person pushes back. But if you don't push, the other person doesn't either. It's instinctive, but not widely understood.

You may be tempted to start explaining to dissatisfied customers why it is that the product is as it is. Don't. This doesn't work either. Nobody wants to hear a lecture on why he is wrong. As Stephen M Covey advocated, in *The 7 Habits of Highly Effective People*, 'In order to be understood, seek first to understand.' In other words, don't tell people what to expect. Make sure you know what they want, and be sure that's what you are giving them.

Some years ago, I went to a fashionable new restaurant that promised appetising food from a small menu. The chefs had estimated how much they needed to cook, but, by the time we came to order, three of the starters and two of the main courses were unavailable. We soldiered on – the food, to be fair, was really quite good – and we made our complaint about the lack of choice available to us at the end.

To my amazement, there was no apology, no understanding of our disappointment. The response was just that this was how it was. Tough luck, in effect. The owner didn't even seem interested in getting us to come back and try the place again some other time. We took the hint and never returned, and the restaurant folded within the year.

This course of action is not completely foolproof. Nothing is. You will sometimes lose customers. Everyone does. But if you take my advice, the only customers you'll lose are that special group of people for whom nothing is ever good enough. You know them. They're the ones who complain that it's your fault the goods didn't make it through the sudden blizzard in time. It's important to realise, though, that very few customers are actually like that – and it's not helpful to assume that many are. Nor is it much fun. If selling seems like a battle, if it's hard to persuade people of the benefits you're offering them, it's time to take a good look at what you're selling and how you're selling it:

▸ You may be failing to sell the benefits and getting bogged down explaining features.

▸ You may be trying to do something you don't enjoy, which would be better done by someone else.

Even if you're convinced you're right and you win a court case to prove it, you will be worse off overall than using your money and energy to fix it – or even agreeing to disagree and giving the disgruntled customer a refund.

Stick with your basic strategy – explaining the benefits you provide, consistently delivering a good product, making reasonable promises and fulfilling them. If it's not working, investigate why and fix it. Don't try something else until either you have fixed it or stopped doing it.

It may sound obvious, but I have seen businesses that have had a good launch rush to create another product before they have made an impact with the first. Momentum is good. That's what you want. Momentum means you have a profitable product that is becoming highly regarded and getting a life of its own. Until you can see that, you don't yet have something you can grow.

Spreading the word

If you are selling a product that's good, you will get positive customer reactions, which you can then use to publicise your product further. Customer quotes carry weight, but they are vastly more effective when they are attributed. I came across a business once that refused to put any named customer feedback on its website for fear of losing customers to its competitors. Oddly enough, it hadn't grown. I persuaded the company to put the names up (with the customers' permission) on the grounds that it was highly unlikely that these happy customers, of all people, would defect to a competitor.

In the past, it used to cost companies a lot of money to spread these validating testimonials around to other potential customers. But the internet has slashed the cost enormously, by 99% according to some estimates. You can put these customer quotes up on your website and refer to them in discussion groups, at conferences, in publications, and on TV and radio shows if your story is big enough to interest the broadcast media. You don't usually need PR consultants. I would only recommend using them if you are sure they know your industry and its influential writers and opinion formers and you don't.

> Momentum means you have a profitable product that is becoming highly regarded and getting a life of its own

You can also work to spread the word face to face, through your sales pitches and networking. In a recent survey, people were asked what frightened them the most in life.

You may have seen the poll results in the press.

Death came third! Above it on the list, the two most frightening things in today's world, according to this large research study, were:

- ▸ Speaking in public (this is sometimes known as a sales pitch).

- ▸ Going into a room full of strangers (this is also known as a networking event).

You may have handed these areas over to your partner. But if not, or if you would like to try it yourself first, there are some simple rules that will make it easier.

1. To give a coherent sales pitch:

   a. Practise the opening sentence or two and get them off pat, word for word. By having a clear starting thought, you will create a hook to remember the rest of your points. Without it, your mind will probably go blank, and that will feel like a nightmare.

   b. Memorise it until you know what is on the next slide *before* it appears.

   c. When the potential customer wants to get to know you or is engaged (and understands the benefits), tell stories. Our brains remember stories easily, even if you're just telling the story of how and why the product came into being. Stories provide memory hooks for your listeners and get you remembered. Their appeal is individual and emotional, all of which aids getting your name known. Would you remember to compare the market without a nudge from that infuriating meerkat?

2. Know the rules of networking events. Everyone there is in roughly the same boat and most of them will welcome you if you walk up to them and catch their eye. Some will ignore you, but it's not personal. No problem, just try somewhere else. It's far better to talk than to stand there trying to look busy with your Blackberry or the event programme. Start the conversation the same way you start sales meetings, by asking about the people you're meeting and listening to their answers. After practising a few times, you'll get the hang of it. And don't worry. The people you didn't get it right with won't remember you at all.

Making proper use of your customer recommendations and networking opportunities should generate sales by word of mouth. But you can also build up sales, sometimes very quickly, by using distributors.

Distribution

Distributors exist in every market, not just those where there are people called 'distributors'.

In the case of FD Solutions, my experience had taught me that people with financial problems go to banks, lawyers, accountants and venture capitalists. So I went to people with jobs in these areas and told them I was available for hire, in the hope that they would 'distribute' me. But very few of them were interested in my services or able to convince their clients to use me. I call those that can do this sort of thing C.O.W.s, because they have the three qualifications of capability, opportunity and willingness. These elements are quite closely related to the trust equation we looked at in Chapter 3:

▸   Capability means they are good enough at their jobs, reliable and close enough to their clients or customers to be trusted, so their recommendations are likely to be followed.

▸   Opportunity means they deal with clients or customers and aren't in senior management positions where they don't meet many of their customers, the people who might need your services.

▸ Willingness means they understand that recommending someone who is suitably capable is a good thing. They'll be seen to be acting in the client's best interests, rather than being purely self-oriented, and this will win them greater trust.

Without distributors, knowing or unknowing, even the best ideas are unlikely to take off.

Multimaps was an invention that produced 3D maps of ski resorts, a brilliant idea which was really useful and could be produced economically, so it could make a profit at a low retail price. All the company needed to do was get it to the customers. The points of sale were many – ski lifts, tourist offices and shops in the ski resorts, and tour company offices. Multimaps made initial sales to them, but never sold enough to be viable, because it couldn't create any C.O.W.s.

▸ Tour companies and shops wanted items with higher value, and high profits, such as weekly ski passes.

▸ The resorts had their own 2D maps, which were much less clear and interesting but free.

All these potential outlets were capable of selling the new maps and had customers passing through their premises every day. But none of them was willing to distribute the new Multimaps product, and the company, inevitably, er... folded.

You may need to add a financial incentive, but this is not always the case. In professional services, for example, it is often enough for referrers or distributors to be seen to have introduced you. It shows they have the client's welfare at heart and so the client is more positive towards them. In some cases, people in professional services roles will be hoping you'll return the favour and recommend them.

But financial incentives – commissions or referral fees – are quite common, especially where the relationship is transactional, like the buying and selling of consumer goods.

In working out the amount you should pay the distributor, remember you're not going to be able to add this on to the sale price. It's going to have to come off your profit margin, because the sale price has been set in competition with other products on the market, and the involvement of a distributor can't change that. The right amount to offer may be easily calculated. If you're selling through retailers, they will be looking for a profit that's in line with what they make on other competing products. If not, you'll need to negotiate a deal that gives both parties what they need. You are looking for increased volume. What the distributor is looking for will vary – better products, wider range, more profit, who knows? It may be worth asking, straight out, what the distributor would like to achieve by working with you. In the end, what you need is a distribution agreement that provides what the distributor wants, in return for more volume for you. Win-win always works best, so you want to create an incentive for the distributor to help you. The key considerations in these agreements are:

▶ **Exclusivity:** If you are asked to agree to sell only through one distributor, you need a minimum order quantity, covering every year of the agreement. This is dangerous territory, as the distributor may not pay you and you won't have the funds to sue for non-payment, even if you were paid up front for the initial order. Having all your eggs in one basket leaves you very vulnerable to any change of mind or policy shift. This is rare in the home market, because the distributor will probably not be your only outlet, but quite a common problem if you're exporting (which we shall deal with later).

▶ **Promotion:** You need a fair amount of space on your distributor's shelves or in the brochure, at least comparable with any competing products. Anything else, such as a launch promotion, will have to be paid for by both of you, either upfront or by reducing your price further.

▶ **Support:** This agreement is only the start. You need to make sure the distributor's staff on the ground will be informed or trained, so that they understand what they are selling, and are enthusiastic. Go and see them if you can, so you can help them appreciate what may, at first, look like just another product, like all the rest.

What isn't in these agreements, but is also important, is that you need to pull as well as push. The distributor's presence is helpful for you – people go to Waitrose because they know they will be able to get the products there that they want – but you can't push your products through a distributor without pulling them through, too. You must continue active marketing yourself, and keep on steering potential customers towards the distributor's outlets.

> You need to pull as well as push

Managing resources

Kevin came to see me once and said he was seriously thinking of giving up his new venture, a brilliant product based on creating 3D videos for insurers to help them mount a defence against unwarranted claims for injuries in car crashes. I said that I had thought of giving up on FD Solutions on three separate occasions.

'You? But you're successful,' Kevin exclaimed. Maybe, but I had to keep going for many years – through downs, as well as ups – to achieve my overnight success.

There are two reasons why you need to just hang on, hang in and husband your resources for a while:

1. Remember your original thinking. You're solving a problem that's either not so severe and experienced by many, or that's

quite severe but experienced by a few. It takes time to either persuade the many that this is the solution or to find the few that experience it.

2. The UK is a conservative society, and people tend to hang on to their wealth, either actively or subliminally. Getting Brits to change their habits is hard. Contrast this with the US, which still thinks of itself as the land of opportunity, or with emerging economies, where change happens much faster. In some of these countries, where income per head is perhaps a tenth of that in the UK, new products represent opportunities for change and are therefore more desirable than here.

Of the three resources at your disposal – time, money and people – time is the most precious **at this stage**. This means that, at this stage, you should avoid increasing production capacity beyond the demand you can see 'plus one'. Only when it's time to expand should you mobilise significant resources. I'll explain when that is in the next Chapter.

Rather than spending on recruitment, premises and a lot of different forms of marketing, spend your money on small amounts of marketing and see what produces results (which you can repeat when it's time to expand) and earmark new people to come on board when the time is right. You may fail to recruit a few good people when sales orders don't materialise and they get themselves other jobs, you may miss out on some sales, but at least your business will still be intact. When you can see an order that will increase revenues for several months ahead, that's the time when you can take someone on to support or deliver it and to start looking for the next growth increment. If that next increment doesn't appear and you have excess capacity again, cut your payroll. This may not mean losing people. You may find that your staff will agree to work for a small or much reduced salary for a while. Like you, they may want to make a difference, and find that working to build the business satisfies that need in them.

> At this stage, you should avoid increasing production capacity beyond the demand you can see 'plus one'

> While growing FD Solutions, I reduced the risk of running out of resources by paying basic salaries of just 60% of the market rate. I gave big bonuses to make up some of the shortfall, but people were still working for less than they could earn elsewhere. They did, however, get a real sense of engagement and the satisfaction of knowing that our work was really useful, as we could make a big difference to many of our clients.

Be careful about offering shares to bridge the gap between what you can afford and what your early employees would like. Some people will see this as 'funny money', even though you see it as the greatest gift. At this stage, I'd be surprised if you had more than three shareholders.

If you're doing the other things right – such as increasing sales by spreading the word – increased demand will follow. We will look at how to build up to a more substantial workforce, and where you'll find the funding to pay these new people, in the next chapter.

The only way to succeed consistently is to think win-win

Negotiating

As the development of your idea begins to involve more people, all demanding their share of this new cake, you will need to negotiate with them in order to grow your sales and profits. There are any number of books on the topic of negotiation, but my guidance, based on long experience, is based on three key points:

1. The only way to succeed consistently is to think win-win. In the introduction to this book, I said that only those who know how to win are suitable for WealthBeing and that is true. But knowing how to win is not the same as insisting on winning every time, regardless of the longer-term consequences. You also need to remember to act in ways that are consistent with your

own morality. By being committed to integrity and fairness, you should end up with agreements in which both parties win, most of the time – though, of course, none of us adheres to these principles perfectly. Try to steer clear of situations where either you, or the person on the other side of the negotiation, is destined to lose.

2. To make sure you don't lose, be absolutely sure that the other side is committed to giving something back. It's all too easy to come to an agreement in which you do X and the other side *may* then do Y. This is not the sort of agreement you want to be part of. If you can't see any tangible commitment in relation to a particular point, disregard it in shaping the deal.

After I'd been trading for a while, I was asked by an ex-employer if I would contract with him, too. He was known as an aggressive negotiator who always kept looking for more and more from a deal – and lost many as a result. In practice, those deals he won often had a sting in the tail. The other party would appear to concede everything he wanted, but that would be because there was some other factor he hadn't considered.

I offered him the same deal I offer all our clients, based on payment by the hour for time worked. This is potentially a win-win scenario, as long as the work is defined properly and the time spent is regarded as reasonable, and we still maintain this approach. I explained to him that a fixed fee necessarily means there will always be a winner and a loser, so I did not want to take that route. When he insisted, apparently relishing the idea that business was a war in which one side would always win at the other's expense, I decided I didn't want to work with him and declined his invitation to continue negotiating.

Be aware of what your bottom line is and don't go below it. When you hit your limit, say so, rather than avoiding concluding the negotiations.

3.   Finally, expect the unexpected. It's an axiom of military strategists that no battle plan survives the first contact with the enemy, and I can't recall a single negotiation plan that has survived unchanged past the first contact with the other side. You may think you know where the other party is coming from, but you don't know this person that well and it's highly likely that he or she will bring in something you haven't thought of. If you have a plan and simply follow it (either explicitly, putting all your cards on the table, or implicitly, by leading the conversation), you will find it hard to end up where you want to be. If, instead, you keep your plan at the back of your mind, but allow the other person to set out his or her thoughts, you can navigate around them to get to your intended position, or as close as possible to it.

In 2009, at the height of the recession, we were following up an important lead. Given the level of trade at that time, we were extremely keen to land this deal, and I was prepared to sacrifice significant margin to get it. My colleagues and I agreed, in advance of the meeting, that we would quote a low price, if it was necessary to win the business. When the client arrived, we listened to his requirements and demonstrated our capabilities, which closely matched his needs. He was obviously impressed, and said: 'It's clear to me you guys know exactly what you're doing. We'd like to go ahead. What price do you charge?' Recognising that this was a positive buying signal, I shelved the idea of dropping the price and quoted our full rate, which was accepted without further discussion.

Culture and infrastructure

If you're going to create a substantial business that you can sell, it needs to be able to function and expand. Some people call this scalability, and it's a key part of the 'glue' that I referred to when we were talking about selecting a partner or mentor. There are two elements to it:

1. The backbone is processes, which ensure good quality every time, including putting mistakes right.

2. There must also be a culture that ensures adherence to the processes while the situation remains unchanged and a readiness to improve them as circumstances alter.

When I was building FD Solutions, my staff often asked me 'What should I do?' My answer was always the same: 'Make sure it's right.' That doesn't sound very helpful, does it? But it is the underlying principle in creating culture and processes. It was essential that my people knew the principles and objectives that drove the business and were prepared to take responsibility for acting in line with them, without always needing specific instructions from me.

Manuals, procedures, forms and now workflows are the bane of all our lives, but they are as necessary as they are undesirable. To create them and make them work for you, make sure you fully understand how the product is manufactured or your service is provided, and write it down.

In order to get this clear understanding, try performing all the processes yourself. It's generally easy to write down how a process should happen. What is harder is dealing with the exceptions, so that it can work always, not just most of the time. Keep track of exceptions and ask yourself 'Ah yes, that's OK – but what if... ?' Always stay open to the possibility that the system doesn't work, even when those who designed it tell you it

Accept mistakes as learning processes

does. They will always say this, because it's one of those situations we referred to earlier, where you are pushing their hand and they will push back as a natural reflex.

To reduce the instances of system failure – 'Computer says no' – make sure that your systems are not unnecessarily prescriptive. If your staff feel that there is no room for them to make any decisions and exercise their judgement, they will feel disempowered and demotivated. Systems should ensure that the individual (sales person, deliverer or installer) reaches the customer fully equipped to do what the customer expects, but with sufficient freedom to do what the customer actually wants. If you hear phrases like 'I'd like to give you a refund, but the system won't let me', then you have too much control in the system. Misusing refunds, giving them out when they are not justified, is an obvious way of cheating the company, but it's better for a few unjustified refunds to be made than for the company to get a bad reputation for customer service. Your systems should flag up any unexpectedly high level of refunds from a particular person. You can then address the issue with the employee involved, after the customers have gone.

If your staff are going to make good decisions most of the time, you need a culture that promotes this – one that's based on collaboration, that allows problems to be referred upwards and that accepts mistakes as learning processes, and fixes them. You can create this kind of culture by consistently using the sort of language that supports it. Here are some examples:

IF YOU WANT TO:	DON'T SAY:	DO SAY:
Accept mistakes:	Why did you do that?	We all make mistakes. Do you remember when I went to the client's office while the client came to meet me here?
Be seen to be supportive:	I can't. I'm busy.	What do you need?
Be part of a team, acting co-operatively not unilaterally:	I believe this is right.	My view is… What do you think?

As always, this entails using questions rather than statements as the way to communicate. To make sure problems don't drag on, with everyone continuing to ask endless questions of each other, train people to work towards ending each incident in one of three ways, which I call the 3As:

▸ **Agreement** Be explicit. Don't just nod and act, but say what you agree with.

▸ **Acceptance** Even though I don't agree, you have heard my views and since you are the senior person here, I will accept your decision.

▸ **Amendment** We have discussed it and moved on from where we started to this position.

There will still sometimes be miscommunication, so keep checking that people are clear about what has been agreed.

I once sent an invoice to Gordon Durham & Co and wrote on it, 'Don't pay until I say so.' I thought that was plain enough, and I had my own reasons for wanting to delay the payment for a while. But I still got a call a couple of days later from the MD. Despite my note, he was obviously keen to stick to the company's normal routine of paying invoices promptly. 'I've got Dave (the company accountant) with me,' he said. 'Can we pay this invoice of yours now?'

It is vital to make sure that you don't have energy sappers in your organisation. Working out how things should be organised to keep customers happy without exhausting your staff or breaking the rules is difficult enough. You don't need people telling you it can't be done, or saying this to others behind your back, or just revelling in doing everything so differently that you wonder if they ever listened to a word you said.

Dr Sharon Turnbull, a leading expert on organisations and leadership, believes you should look at the people who work for you in terms of two dimensions: committed/uncommitted and critical/uncritical. She has defined six key groups, each with distinctive attitudes:

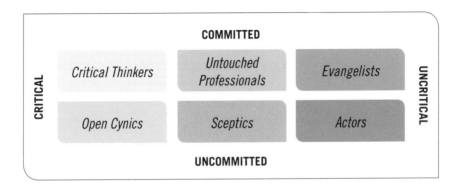

The key group here is the critical thinkers, those who don't accept what you say at face value but think about it rationally and test it to see if it will work.

If you work closely with them and put them in positions of authority, they will help you to build a growing organisation with a positive and durable culture. As their influence spreads, you will see sceptics becoming committed, evangelists learning that the original idea may have needed tweaking and actors (those who pretended to agree) and even open cynics (those who were prepared to risk their jobs in order to be heard) becoming committed to getting things done, rather than saying 'It'll never work.'

Now that you have created a culture, you'll have to keep working on it for as long as you're involved with the business. It may be a cliché to say 'Culture eats strategy for breakfast', but it's absolutely true. I'm reminded of a conversation I once had with the CEO of a successful FTSE 350 company. Her problem, she said, was that, having devised and implemented a successful strategy, she was still left with one overriding issue – the organisation's culture. My own, slightly mischievous, view is that, for many people, in many different organisational cultures, there are only two rules about following rules:

1. They don't apply to me.

2. If they do, they don't apply in these circumstances.

If you find this aspect of business as hard to handle as I do, maybe you, too, should hand it over to someone else.

Now that you have created a culture, you'll
have to keep working on it for as long as
you're involved with the business

WealthBeing check

Wealth

The nurturing stage will take one, two or three years, maybe more. Your annual results will look something like this:

PROFIT AND LOSS ACCOUNTS

Activity	Item	£'000	Comments
Trading	Sales	300.0	
	Cost of Sales	-150.0	
Gross profit		**150.0**	
Staff	Office Support	-75.0	2–3 people (including NI) & £10,000 to you
Marketing	Travel & Subsistence	-15.0	
	Website	-5.0	Maintenance and minor modifications
Premises	Office	-15.0	For 3–5 people
IT/Comms	Laptop & Software	-5.0	
	Phones & Internet	-6.0	
Admin	Insurance	-1.5	Basic package plus specific liability
	Bookkeeping	-5.0	Still essential!
	Sundries	-2.5	
Profit/(loss) before tax		**20.0**	
Distribution	Tax	-0.3	@ 20% of profit less accumulated losses
	Dividend to you	-10.0	Above £10,000 you save tax paying a dividend rather than salary
Retained in the business		**9.7**	

And your balance sheet will look something like this:

BALANCE SHEETS

Item	£'000	Comments
Fixed Assets	**.0**	**Don't be tempted to acquire stuff. Cash is king.**
Debtors	**100.0**	**Sales are growing and so will debtors**
Creditors	**-70.3**	**You can get reasonable credit now**
Working Capital	29.7	This is the net amount of debtors who owe you and creditors whom you owe. It is a sizeable figure, three times your annual profit
Cash at Bank	**0.1**	**Profits, yes, but cash is used up funding the working capital**
Loan From You	-38.5	In addition to a basic salary and dividend you can repay some loan
Net Assets	**-8.7**	
Share Capital	0.1	
P&L Account	-8.8	
Net Worth	**-8.7**	

The essence of a business that has been nurtured is that some good things begin to occur without you making them happen. Customers come back with repeat orders and new customers get in touch because they have heard about you on the grapevine. You'll have a small group of people who understand what the product is there to do and are enjoying making a difference to people's lives by delivering it. Sales will be unpredictable, but your business will already be looking like a 'real' business. Cash is still tight, but the business is looking after you while you are looking after it.

Wellbeing

It's taken quite some time to get here, longer than you thought. Maybe you have discovered a degree of resilience you didn't know you had. You know you are providing something useful and new and the surge of energy you feel when someone contacts you and asks you to meet their needs is inspiring. The reward for putting your reputation, skills and character on the line to be judged by others is to have them validated, to be told, 'Yes, you're good enough to satisfy me.' This should give you a growing confidence in your own abilities, and make you feel (you've guessed it) good.

WealthBeing

▬▬ Wealth
▬▬ Being

Before **50** 50

Create **45** 60

Launch **25** 25

Nurture **25** 50

It's probably inevitable that the hours and effort required to make things work consistently well will sometimes break into your leisure time. Combined with the stress of uncertainty, not knowing whether it will work or not, this will almost certainly have taken its toll on you physically. Remember, though, that achieving WealthBeing is about getting you to feel well, as well as wealthy. Your diet, exercise and sleep will probably have suffered and you must focus, or refocus, on getting them back into balance. A successful growing business is one with a fit boss, and I can't think of one successful entrepreneur who isn't energetic. It's this vitality, even more than your ability to execute, that will ensure success on the remainder of your journey to WealthBeing.

5

EXPANDING IT

Introduction

Growing sales to this kind of level, with very few people involved, has meant concentrating on execution. You've been focusing on getting the product quality, customer satisfaction and infrastructure right, finding premises (not too large and on flexible terms), introducing IT (using standard software), recruiting customers and ensuring suppliers are paid on time – and eventually getting to the stage where you can pay yourself (in the form of a salary, dividends or loan repayments). But then what? Do you hire more sales people? Get a larger space to expand into? Create a share scheme? The options can be bewildering.

It's also almost invariably the case that the business is taking up more and more of your life. This is generally born out of the notion that if you keep doing what you've been doing, sales will increase and so will profits, unless you spend money on more people. This leads on to the assumption that the way to succeed is to do everything yourself, which you have proved that you can do. But this is not how you will achieve WealthBeing. You won't be able to sell the business until you have capable people around you. And even if you get a lot of energy from working in the business, spending too much time on it will, eventually, lead to a loss of perspective that can damage your other relationships and may suddenly leave you facing the problems of burn-out.

It's easy to fall into this trap – always saying 'We can't afford it', and failing to advance for fear that you will lose what you've gained. But it is now clear that you have created something people really do want and the business is starting to take off. Your priorities are changing, and you are quickly moving from being cash poor to being time poor.

How can you tell that this is what's going on? By trial and error: do it and see what happens.

By 1998, I was getting busy, acting as finance director to six or seven companies, and 50–60 hour working weeks were becoming the norm. I knew it was time to employ someone else. I also knew that, besides the requirement to pay a salary, this would itself take up time, for recruitment, training and supervision. But without this investment there was no way of growing. So we employed Ian. He started on Monday morning and by the afternoon I had already arranged to take him to a client. By Wednesday of that week, he was fully booked. So we employed Gordon, another FD, and found that within four weeks he, too, was busy. From that point on, growth was always a question of looking at the current situation, checking everything was working well, and then taking a step into the unknown.

The current numbers, however well prepared and detailed they are, will never provide conclusive evidence that it's right to gear up for further expansion. But the fact that what you are doing is working is sufficient evidence, in itself, to justify adding some more capacity.

If you find you've added too much extra capacity, there will usually be a number of ways to backtrack a bit until growth picks up again.

In early 2009, the corporate finance-based work we had done in the boom times had disappeared and hadn't yet been replaced by turnaround work in the wake of the financial crisis. The banks were just allowing companies to continue in breach of their covenants, because their new political masters didn't want the embarrassment of mass insolvencies, and we found ourselves with surplus capacity. Rather than dismantle our team with a round of redundancies, we took the view that the downturn was cyclical and unlikely to be prolonged. So we asked our people to forgo their bonuses and work four days a week, initially for a period of three months. Everyone could see the wisdom of this approach and the common response was 'If you think that's the best thing to do, we should do it.' By the autumn of 2009, the first green shoots were appearing, and by 2011 sales and salaries were back to normal.

Adopting the right principles and structure will play a vital part in keeping your plans on track. I recommend that you pay particular attention to the points listed here:

1. You need to change your relationship with the business, let go of executive responsibility and **become a leader.**

2. You can then **recruit and motivate people** who buy in to the vision and values.

3. **Expand your sales.** Have a clear message on which to base your conversations and avoid the temptation to 'shout'.

4. Develop the **appropriate business model** – direct or indirect sales, licensing or franchising.

5. **Stay profitable.** As you grow, you will need support and assistance. Sometimes the cost of this outweighs the value you are creating, but this need not be the case.

6. As the wealth checks in the last two chapters have shown, there is a significant difference between transacting business and getting paid. Manage the balance sheet to **create positive cashflow.**

7. You will undoubtedly encounter **problems** along the way, and we will look at ways of dealing with them.

Again, we will end this chapter with a WealthBeing check, so that you can see the progress that is being made.

Becoming a leader

You may think that creating your product and selling it is the hardest thing about business. But as you develop yourself and the enterprise, you learn how to do this, and may become so happy that you are in flow. *Flow* is the name of a book by psychologist Mihaly Csíkszentmihályi (the full title is actually *Flow: The Classic Work on How to Achieve Happiness*), in which he identified four elements of activity that produce happiness:

1. Concentrating on an activity that requires skill, has a clear set of goals and is bounded by rules. Producing your product fits this description.

2. Possessing the skills to be confident of achieving your task, but not finding it too easy, so that you feel engaged. Each successful presentation or improvement in the service demonstrates this.

3. Focusing hard, so there is no room for anything else, including unpleasant thoughts and excuses. When this happens, you lose track of time. You may appear committed and sometimes even workaholic, but the truth is you love the work you're doing.

4. Getting clear and immediate feedback, or being able to check progress quickly and simply. An order or a new enquiry would fit the bill.

The result is what Csíkszentmihályi calls a feeling of 'union with the environment' and an 'enrichment of the sense of self'.

This is a great place to be, of course. But feeling good like this is not enough to achieve WealthBeing. Until there are other people involved near the top of the company, in proper managerial and directorial roles, you won't grow the business much or be able to sell it. A growing business that is going to be bought by someone else must have a capable management team and no longer be relying on its founder. You may know, logically, that this is true. But you will also need to overcome your emotional fears about letting go and trusting your employees, even though you're probably worried that they might get things wrong and that the business may suffer.

The solution is to give them practice at getting things wrong, and learning from their mistakes, well before the time when you will be letting go of the reins. You can introduce these things gradually, without the business suffering. Delegate tasks, at first, but not responsibility. For the first few weeks, repeat instructions, check everything in detail and ask people how they're doing. Then, when they're ready for it,

Overcome your emotional fears about letting go

let them carry on, on their own. Look for the positive contribution they are making or will make (even if it takes a few months). Even if they lose some sales you'd have hoped to get, you may find the business is better off overall, because the overall sales total has gone up since these people have been doing more.

This kind of leadership, enabling, empowering and encouraging people to perform, is absolutely essential if the business is to grow. It will reward you emotionally, too, because it fulfils some of the Hierarchy of Needs Maslow pointed to – esteem (from being independent not just of an employer but of the company's daily routine), self-actualisation (realising all, not just some, of your potential), and transcendence (by giving you the time and capability to guide others). Ideally, you will experience flow in your role as a leader:

1. Building an organisation has a clear goal and is bounded by rules.

2. You probably have sufficient skills to do this. If you're not sure, sign up for a management course. It should be built around the basic disciplines of good leadership – vision, values and the skill of making balanced judgements about people's performance.

3. If you take to these, you will become lost in the moment as you apply them and discover the joys of growing a business by leading, rather than doing.

4. As you apply your new techniques, you'll win the appreciation and loyalty of your staff, and maybe even of customers and suppliers too.

Management, which consists of organising resources (including people) to achieve particular outcomes, is a key part of the leader's role.

But if leadership, management and creating structure make you feel uncomfortable, if you would rather be busy doing and in flow than be managing other people, you have a choice. It's your company. Create the role that will suit you best – maybe key account salesman or technical director – and employ others to bring in the support and assistance you need to fill in the gaps. This could be your business partner or even be a managing director. There's no reason why your business can't be led by someone else and still maintain its momentum.

It's simple. If you don't want to manage, employ a manager. If you don't like structure, get an efficient PA to deal with the structural aspects of your role. This approach will not only ensure an effective and well-balanced organisation, but also serve to maintain your wellbeing.

To create a successful business, you need to keep all the plates spinning and make sure every aspect is performing well. In the early days, the only way of doing this is usually to attend to every little thing yourself. Beyond a certain size, this is impossible. And if you're not growing to the size you expected, this may actually be because you have been failing to delegate.

> To create a successful business, you need to keep all the plates spinning

I found an answer to this by constantly reminding myself 'The less I do, the more I get done.' It's a useful phrase to encourage you to delegate more. And when you do let go, it's amazing how much others can do.

Recruiting and managing a team

The extent to which you can enable others to perform, without actually organising them yourself, varies according to the situation and your feelings. Sometimes you will feel compelled to give specific instructions or wish that you had got involved sooner. You can't get it right every time. But the more you can lead, and the more hands-off you can be when you manage, the more successful your business will be. When you start to find that there is no need for you or your partner to issue instructions to get the right result from, say, the marketing team, at the end of the month, you will

> You can't get it right every time

know the company is starting to run itself. The time you've invested – first in doing and then in managing – is paying off, because you no longer need to do either, leaving you free to concentrate on generating further growth. To help you reach this happy state of affairs, there are five principles to bear in mind:

1. Hire for attitude.

2. Build a team with complementary skills and attributes.

3. Enhance peoples' existing skills, rather than insisting they develop new ones.

4. Manage, don't meddle.

5. Manage with reference to a vision and a set of values.

Hire for attitude

When you're recruiting people, it is natural to focus on what they are going to do. We usually recognise that they also need to fit in, but there is never a perfect candidate who scores 100% on all counts, so compromises have to be made. The big question is how to choose between someone who has great qualifications and experience and someone with little experience who is extremely positive.

The quick fix is usually to hire the more experienced candidate, in the hope that this person will slot quickly and easily into the role you have in mind. In my experience, that is often the wrong decision.

Skills can be learned, especially by someone who is enthusiastic (just remember the committed/critical matrix in Chapter 4 and check that they are not acting or too easily persuaded). Attitudes are much slower to change, however hard you try to sell the company culture to your new staff member. It's easier to change what someone does than to change the person. You are a new company with a new product, too, so experience with similar products may not even be an advantage. Experienced people are often likely to be attached to the conventional ways of doing the job. But what you need is someone who is keen to adopt and spread the new gospel.

No selection process is infallible. A person can show a good attitude at interview and change their tune later, and employers' references are virtually meaningless these days – everyone is scared stiff that an employee who's been given a bad reference will kick up a fuss and threaten to take legal action. So what can you do?

My advice is to use LinkedIn to identify some ex-colleagues of the person you are hiring – people who used to work with the candidate, but are no longer working for that employer – and get in touch with them. They will feel free to make more candid comments and you are

> People who feel good work well

bound to find at least one who will give you an honest assessment. If no-one is prepared to do that, you can draw your own conclusion – that nobody has a good word to say about this person.

You need people who feel good working in your business. As I've said, it's people's emotional state that drives action. Only people who feel good work well. That's not the whole story, of course, because not everyone who feels well works well. But if they are directed and managed properly, these are the people who can help you make your business flourish.

Build a team

Teams need to be competent in all the functional business areas such as sales, marketing, production, finance, IT and HR. But they also need to bring together a range of attributes and attitudes that will enable the team to make the right decisions and implement them correctly. There are many psychometric tests that can help you discover how a potential employee is likely to respond to situations and approach new problems. My personal favourite is the Myers-Briggs Type Indicator®, a tried and tested personality assessment tool which has been in use since 1962. Myers-Briggs testing used to be available only via qualified and certificated coaches, but it's now there online for anyone to use, free of charge, albeit without expert guidance. The test looks at four dimensions of personality and assesses whether someone tends towards either analytical or intuitive/emotional behaviour in each of them:

1. Where the team member gets his energy – from inside himself (introvert) or from those around him (extrovert)?

2. How she takes in and processes information – by looking at it literally or getting an intuitive feel for, say, the numbers?

3. How he makes decisions – by analysing a problem and deducing what should be done or by getting a feel for what is the right decision?

4. How she orientates herself to the world generally – does she make plans for the day and stick to them or take lunch where and when she feels like it?

Clearly there is no right answer. Companies tend to err towards the apparent certainties of logical, analytical thinking, but there are many situations in business where you are operating on incomplete information. Unquoted companies like yours don't face the plc's imperative to keep making decisions to satisfy shareholders' expectations of quarterly growth, but decisions are still needed. A logical, Spock-type individual may be totally flummoxed and paralysed by not having all the facts, while a more intuitive person may still be able to grasp the overall situation and make good decisions. To manage the business successfully, your team needs a mix of different types so that all the bases are covered. If you happen to be an extrovert, the business will benefit from having an introvert in the team who notes down what you say and carries it out. If you make decisions on the hoof, intuitively, without getting bogged down in all the details, it will be helpful to have someone alongside you who can examine your proposals in the light of the facts and make sure that they are workable.

Enhance existing skills

People with the right attitude will happily acquire the skills they need to perform effectively. If they don't get up to speed quickly, you can move them to different roles that let them play to their strengths. If it turns out that someone can generate leads but can't close sales, get this person to focus on making the initial contact with potential customers. If you have someone who gets impatient with simple, repetitive customer queries, move this person into a second-tier support role, where he or she can get stuck in and gain satisfaction from helping customers with some of their more difficult and challenging problems.

Coaches often refer to the mantra that says 'Be who you really are.' But what does that really mean? Aren't we already real? What the coaches are getting at is the simple truth that people are most effective when they're doing things they do well and enjoy. Put like that, it doesn't sound like much of an insight. But it's common enough in business to see people being pushed into roles that don't suit them. Why take your best salesman off the road and make him a director? Why ask your quiet accountant to make a key presentation to the bank? It's presumably because you think that they are doing a good job now and can probably make a successful switch to the new role.

That doesn't always follow. They may want to progress and try different things. If so, you must set out the skills and attributes needed and make sure that both of you agree that these can be acquired. But if that doesn't happen, you'll have to find someone else who already has the skills needed for the new role. And when growth is really dramatic, you may prefer to hire for tomorrow. If sales are likely to double this year, find yourself a sales director who has managed the projected sales volume, rather than your current level. That person will cost more but should be willing to share the risk by accepting a salary that includes performance-related payments and bonuses. If not, you are probably talking to the wrong candidate.

Management style

It's fine to show people what they have to do and how you do it. But it is counterproductive to insist that people always perform tasks *exactly* the same way you do.

Rather than telling, once again I urge you to lead with questions. We've already talked about the benefits of open questions in helping you make sales and handle negotiations, and they work in management, too. Telling may appear to offer the benefit of unambiguous clarity, but humans are not predisposed to being told what to do all the time. We all have our own issues, mundane or significant, buzzing around in our heads. Even if I appear to be engaged in a task at work, some proportion of my mind is still likely to be taken up with other

> Why take your best salesman off the road and make him a director?

things – what's for supper, how hot the office is and all the rest of them. If you immediately start instructing people, they are unlikely to absorb more than a small part of what you are saying. So ask them how or what they are doing. This makes them more engaged with the task (if they misunderstand or talk about other things, just ask again until they get back to the matter in hand). Then ask them how they could do it differently. You can ask this in an open way or a closed way. Open questions, where the answer is not suggested in the question ('How could you... ?', rather than 'Shouldn't you really... ?') are better because they are more engaging. An open question makes the other person come up with a considered answer, rather than just saying yes or no. The 3As culture that you have created should help here. Remember to get agreement, acceptance or amendment.

Judge people by outcomes – as the legendary basketball coach John Wooden put it, 'Never mistake activity for achievement' – and be on hand to assist when they ask for help.

135

Make sure that you meet up with all your people regularly and that they have a chance to have their say. When you ask a question, make sure you listen closely to the answer (just as if you were selling). You don't need to have all the answers; in fact, it's better if you don't.

Make meetings constructive. There should be a reason for the board to meet, beyond the fact that all companies have board meetings, and a specific agenda that assumes all the relevant information has been looked at beforehand and that will produce decisions to move the company forward.

I'm not being contradictory when I ask you not to make meetings personal. Each person brings his or her own personality to the company and will usually try as hard as possible. As long as people are working in what they perceive to be the best interests of the company, you should assess their contributions objectively and not respond with dismissive comments like 'You would say that' or 'That's what you always say.' What you don't want to see is people working to serve their own self-interest. Having and sharing a vision and a set of values will help to bring out the best in people.

Manage to a vision and a set of values

In the initial stages of building a business, the vision is to achieve survival, by making and selling, and the values are commitment, commitment and more commitment to this basic cause. This is sustainable for a while, but in the long term the business needs something more. It needs a vision that provides an explanation of the benefits it brings to the world, what it believes in and how it organises itself.

Too many visions fall far short of being inspirational. Just exhorting all your stakeholders to increase returns for shareholders by improving the way the business is run is not going to fire people up. An effective vision provides a sense of purpose and a higher, but attainable, goal. In the case of Flexible Directors, what we set out to do was to 'guide ambitious enterprises so as to help them overcome their barriers to growth'. We assess each client each month and see if we are achieving that. Where we do, we feel we are succeeding, and this rationale gives us the energy to do it some more.

As well as clarity about what you do, there needs to be clear agreement about how you do it, to provide the framework for managing your people. This is encapsulated in a set of values, which can be seen as the DNA of a business.

In the beginning, it's possible to start with your own values and recruit people who feel aligned with them. But as the company grows and you move towards leading, rather than executing, it's better for the values to be the result of everybody's input.

One leading expert in this field, Richard Barrett, has done a lot of work on values and has created a helpful website, www.valuescentre.com, which is well worth a visit. He has developed tools you can use, with the help of a qualified practitioner, to explore the values your people believe in, what they consider the current values of your organisation to be and the values they feel would support the company's desired state of being. Barrett uses an anonymous questionnaire that asks people to list their own Top 10 values, followed by those of the company as it is and as they would like it to be. To make sense of the words people choose, each value (covering behaviours like teamworking, as well as moral qualities, such as integrity) is tagged by Barrett and placed on the appropriate level of a model he has constructed, derived from

> Employees understand that they have a job to do... a feeling of togetherness, of being involved jointly in a meaningful enterprise

Maslow's Hierarchy of Needs. If someone chooses the word 'integrity', for example, this indicates that this person has an aesthetic need (for beauty, truth and goodness, in Maslow's terms), which constitutes Level 5 in Barrett's model and covers values such as authenticity and creativity.

As each word is plotted, a pattern emerges of what types of value are important, where the weaknesses are in the organisation and how it needs to change its behaviour if it is to improve and meet the needs of all levels. So, for example, if none of the participants chooses words to describe the organisation that match the Level 5 values, this may imply that people mistrust it and feel it lacks authenticity, though findings like this must always be tested before firm conclusions are drawn.

Of course, it's people, not organisations, who actually exhibit these behaviours. So once a set of values are identified and adopted, you can resolve many issues by reference to them, as an objective and agreed standard. This helps maintain a calmer and more productive atmosphere, which will make it easier to solve all kinds of problems. Just be careful, though, that you adhere to these values, too. There is another Barrett tool that can give you valuable insights into what values you live by and what values others recognise in you. This involves feedback from your staff, which is usually given with the best intentions, and it will help you ensure that your own behaviour clearly demonstrates the values you believe in.

People will work best in a company where they have autonomy and don't face undue interference in their work, where they have mastery and the ability to develop their skills, and where they see a purpose, a vision, a good reason to come in every morning. Fairness is another essential ingredient. In assessing how well off we feel, we all tend to compare ourselves with those who work around us, rather than any statistics.

Pundits often say that for a company to be successful, the people working there need to have fun. I think this is too simple. Employees understand that they have a job to do. What they need is to be able to do that job in a place where there is a feeling of togetherness, of being involved jointly in a meaningful enterprise where things are done well. This is emotionally rewarding and intellectually satisfying in itself, and it can then spill over into fun times, both spontaneously and at organised events.

Expanding sales

In Chapter 4, Nurturing It, we discussed how to spread the word and get others to buy from you. It's possible that this will be enough to build the business to the size you want, but it's very unlikely. Nine times out of ten, the name of the game now will be expanding sales actively. This is often described as pushing sales, rather than relying on them being pulled by word of mouth enquiries. But the internet has almost turned this process upside down. It's easy to get a message out there now, so easy that everyone does it and there are more messages being sent than anyone can receive. As a result, we've all learned to screen most of them out. Marketers are finding that their precious advertising, direct mail and email campaigns are treated as intrusive shouting and pestering and are increasingly ignored.

Your approach can be subtler, cheaper and more effective:

1. Be visible.

2. Have conversations.

3. Build on what has already worked.

4. Be ready to close the sale when appropriate.

Visibility means saying what you do, in all the media that are appropriate. FD Solutions helps ambitious enterprises overcome their barriers to growth, especially cashflow matters. Our website says it, and we use Google AdWords to lead people there. We write blogs about it, appear at conferences and provide free and authoritative material for influential publications that are read by business people. We don't advertise on radio or TV, because they are expensive media aimed at consumers, but we are certainly happy to appear on relevant programmes when we are asked.

> It's easy to get a message out there now, so easy that everyone does it and there are more messages being sent than anyone can receive

We look for customers, too, by applying what I call 'the Amazon principle' – those who bought X also bought Y. It's a very powerful way of expanding your world, and it doesn't require the vast number-crunching capacities of Amazon's monster IT systems. Simple customer relationship management (CRM) software can help you do as we do and comb through all the data you hold – emails, enquiries, records of website hits and lists of names and addresses – to see who has bought from you and to help you find more buyers like that.

Ask people who know you to refer you to people they know. Offer commissions if you like, which can be paid without laying out cash by providing more of your product or service to the referrers.

While there should be many people who need what you can offer, they won't all need it at the same time. You must be prepared to invest in creating awareness for many months before you see significant returns. Sales is a numbers game: the more you do, the more you get back. But until you build up a substantial population of people who know about you, the results will not start to show through.

Getting the distinction right between conversations and closing is tricky. Individual sales people may have a tendency to act one way or the other, so organise your sales team carefully so that there are 'farmers' who nurture customers and 'hunters' who close sales, with the few that can do both managing them.

The other way to expand sales is to present different offerings to your established customers, including add-ons, bundles and 'lite' versions. This is just a matter of continuing your conversations with existing customers, rather than new ones, ensuring that they have a good experience, and finding out what else might be of benefit to them. Some aspects of this can be mechanised – free Survey Monkey questionnaires can be helpful here – but do make sure that you look at the results and demonstrate that you have done so by publicising them.

Developing the business model

The arrangements your company has with its suppliers, customers and end-users (who may be different people) are referred to as your business model. To create a profitable and valuable business, you need to create the best customer model and pay close attention to the supplier model, which may involve getting things made in different ways.

The customer model

In deciding on the right customer model for you, look at three factors:

- ▸ Who is the end user?

- ▸ What existing channels are there that you can use?

- ▸ Could you do better by using different channels?

Successful businesses understand who uses their products, and how. If you're still not sure, now is the time to do some research by surveying as many as possible and interviewing some of them.

There are four types of channel that may be available, apart from direct sales. They are:

1. Distributing through distributors, wholesalers and retailers.

2. Establishing relationships with value-added resellers.

3. Licensing the manufacture and sale of your product.

4. Franchising the whole process.

Most businesses use one of these channels, but few have more than one. Using them means some loss of margin, compared with selling directly, and some loss of control, so you should only pursue these strategies if there is a lot more volume to be won. Avoid exclusive arrangements, unless they are for a short period (two years at the most) and stipulate minimum order quantities, with some cash up front. Otherwise, you run the risk of being strangled at birth.

> Successful businesses understand who uses their products, and how

The last thing you want is a situation where your channel partners have the exclusive right to sell your product but are not doing so – and you can't either. Result, no sales. I also think it's worth sacrificing some margin if they will use this money to promote you, though if the retailer or distributor asks for a price that is at or below your cost price (which can happen), it's definitely time to say no (see Negotiating, p.112).

Logistics have improved in recent years, so the need for distributors, whose main function is to ease stock and delivery constraints, is declining. But the other models continue to provide benefits:

- ▶ Value Added Resellers (VARs) may be able to offer a range of products and the services required to configure them so they work effectively.

- ▶ Manufacturers have their own channels already set up and may be able to use them to achieve large volumes. Setting up the business in this way can potentially maximise returns to the inventor.

- ▶ Franchises can provide you with a presence on the ground in many different locations and reduce the capital needed to expand services that require an infrastructure of vans, branches and people.

There is usually one business model that is obvious for your product and has become the industry standard. Before choosing it, though, see if there are new opportunities available through using a different channel. Would a chain of gyms be suitable for selling sports equipment or a new drink? Would accountancy firms be able to win you new service contracts? Generally the answer is 'No', but if you can find someone you trust and who is interested, or if a potential partner approaches you and is prepared to invest money and effort in making sales a success, this could be a useful adjunct to your existing and direct channels.

Getting things made in a different way

When getting started with a service, it's usual to provide it yourself. As you start to grow, you need to get others to do it, either as well as or instead of you doing it.

It's very unlikely that they will be as capable as you, but you still need to ensure that the customer gets the same service. Rather than passing client relationships on to staff or sub-contractors, delegate the elements that can be delegated and keep the client relationship to yourself. But instead of spending eight hours servicing their needs, spend one hour with the client and at least one hour reviewing the eight hours of work that have been done. You can then either pay the executive at a lower rate than you pay yourself (the rate your own time is costed at) or accept a lower level of profit on this transaction in return for gaining greater capacity.

What you can't do is restrict the total time to the amount of time it used to take you, and expect everything to be as good as it was. The readjustment that is going on here may feel like taking one step back to go two steps forward. It is. As a result, though, the business will develop by continuing to provide a good service, still ultimately approved and presented by you, while being able to handle many more clients.

Once you have got the prototype accepted, you will be able to commence volume runs. If the wrinkles have all been ironed out, this should be easier than commissioning prototypes. But it is still not time to relax. Volumes may have defects which need checking and deadlines must also be clear. You are still a small customer and even an order for 10,000 units won't be that exciting to the supplier, who probably hasn't read *WealthBeing* and isn't aware of the paramount importance of looking after every customer.

If the volume run works well, stick with this supplier. It is likely nowadays that you can get your drink/clothing/tool/gadget made overseas, probably at an enticingly attractive price. But the disadvantages of this still outweigh the advantages. Your inability to inspect and control the process, and the need to pay for your goods in advance, will combine to render you powerless in the event of any production shortcomings. You should only go down this route when you are large enough to have your own member of staff based there, on the ground, to keep an eye on quality and timing.

When it comes to finding your key suppliers, think about the whole venture rather than just the price. A supplier who has similar values to you and understands what you are trying to do is a valuable asset.

I chose Clare Christian and the team at RedDoor to publish *WealthBeing* because they came back to me promptly and showed me they understood what would make the book sell (it's about offering good ideas that people hear about via the usual marketing and social media channels, not access to Waterstones, where you sit alongside ten thousand other books, many with equally attractive covers). Clare has also set up her business model so that even authors can get a decent return on their toil, which was not something that was evident in the other offers I received.

Staying profitable

In Chapter 2, we looked at how you price your goods so that they are profitable even after attributing the appropriate overhead costs to them. But we also acknowledged that there are some costs not directly attributable to sales that are necessary in order to build an infrastructure to support the expansion of the business. These included elements such as IT systems, financial controls, staff contracts and incentives, supply agreements and premises. There is no formula for determining exactly when overheads (the word has rather negative connotations, doesn't it?) should be spent, so this is going to be a matter of business judgement. Jump too soon and you won't make a profit, because the step change of hiring, say, a finance director, is quite large. Leave it too late and you will make mistakes that cost even more to put right.

Rather than taking the risk of committing yourself to these step changes, it is now possible to keep your overheads at just the right level for each stage of your development by acquiring them on flexible terms.

The main item of overhead expenditure is senior staff. It is now possible to hire directors by the hour or the day in every business discipline – including finance, HR, sales, legal, marketing and IT. Why, I could even provide these resources myself! Whoever you choose, though, this approach offers three advantages:

a. You are getting someone very well qualified and probably more capable than a full-time person for the same price. This is because the only way to provide part-time services successfully is to be very good at the job; otherwise you just can't perform.

b. The flexibility of this kind of arrangement means that these people are much easier to manage. This includes terminating their services, if necessary. There won't usually be any employment contracts involved, so the concept of unfair dismissal isn't relevant.

c. The fact that these people are working in other companies means that they will be able to bring in up-to-date ideas from elsewhere, some of which will be useful.

Most of the other services you will need, such as premises, secretarial staff and vehicles, are also available on flexible terms these days. While they may appear more expensive if you gross them up to the equivalent annual rate, they are cheaper for you because you are only paying for what you need. You may hear people say, 'If I had one permanently, it would only cost me £100, so why would I pay £75 to have it half the time?' The reason is starkly simple – £75 is less than £100! If you are only going to use this resource for half the week, it is a waste of money to pay for it 100% of the time.

Cashflow

Losses don't kill businesses, lack of cash does. If you never pay attention to your cashflow, you will go bust one day.

You can sell things at a loss for as long as you want, as long as you have the cash to support this. Thomson Holidays did this for years in the 1980s and 1990s, as it struggled to fight off competition in the package holiday market, and it is still one of the largest package holiday companies (as part of TUI). But if you don't have the cash to support the losses (Thomson Holidays was part of the vast Thomson

Corporation) or you are not generating cash from your activities, the end is nigh.

While losses are fairly obvious and usually lead to prompt action, profits are generally assumed to produce cash. When they don't, it comes as a shock. Even if short-term cashflow problems are understood, because customers will often take time to pay, many business people assume that this problem will resolve itself shortly, because the customers will eventually pay up. But that's a delusion. The fact is that it won't resolve itself, because other customers will also want credit. So desperately needed cash gets 'tied up in working capital', a mysterious phrase I have highlighted in the financial illustrations in my WealthBeing checks. As revenues get up to around the £1 million mark, the business is now approaching the size where working capital and cashflow become a major issue. If they are not managed properly, they can kill it stone dead.

That phrase 'tied up in working capital' signifies that stock, work in progress, product development, new branches, plant and equipment, debtors (people who owe you money) and creditors (people who you owe) all change the cashflow of the business and mean that it does not straightforwardly reflect its profits. What's worse, the more successful you are, the bigger the problem becomes, because more cash is required to finance more sales (to pay your staff and suppliers before your invoice is paid). It is absolutely vital that you know what's happening to your cashflow, on a monthly basis, and that you can reliably predict what is likely to happen over the next three to twelve months. The way to do this is to get an experienced finance director to prepare a spreadsheet that encapsulates the business, the way it works, its results to date and a realistic extrapolation of those results, together with any planned changes, in a way that you and others can understand. It should look something like this:

If you never pay attention to your cashflow, you will go bust one day

PROFIT & LOSS	JUN 12	JUN 13	JUN 14	JUN 15	JUN 16	JUN 17
£'000s	Actual	Forecast	Budget	Budget	Budget	Budget
Revenue	1,515	1,743	2,079	2,290	2,556	2,885
Gross Profit	1,394	1,593	1,927	2,135	2,397	2,723
	92%	91%	93%	93%	94%	94%
People Costs	493	545	553	600	618	637
Expenses	677	767	974	1,186	1,177	1,264
(L)/PBIT	224	281	400	348	602	822
Depreciation	10	18	96	31	43	55
Interest (cost)/income	–	3	–	–	–	–
Corporation Tax	35	17	96	47	116	174
P(L)AT	179	249	207	271	443	594
KPIs						
Year-end Headcount	17	20	22	22	22	22

BALANCE SHEET	JUN 12	JUN 13	JUN 14	JUN 15	JUN 16	JUN 17
Fixed Assets	174	245	909	938	956	961
Curret Assets						
Trade Debtors	53	66	69	76	85	96
Stock	–	–	–	–	–	–
Prepayments	29	34	55	45	45	18
VAT (asset)	–	–	–	–	–	–
Other Debtors	156	256	286	316	346	376
	238	356	410	437	476	490
Current Liabilities						
Trade Creditors	112	71	76	90	90	96
Accruals	11	11	11	11	11	11
PAYE	12	17	19	20	21	21
VAT	47	95	41	49	60	77
Corporation Tax	35	17	96	47	116	174
Other Creditors	38	48	548	548	548	548
	255	259	792	764	845	927
Working Capital Ex Cash	(17)	97	(382)	(327)	(369)	(437)
Cash	93	152	174	361	829	1,485
Net Assets	250	494	701	972	1,416	2,010

PBIT

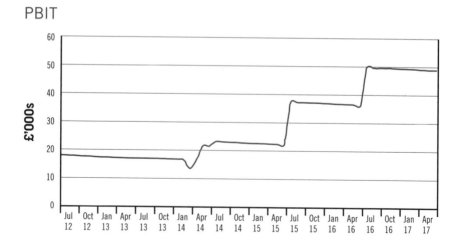

CAPITAL INTRODUCED

	£'000s	Month Debt/Equity
Tranche 1	500	Jan 14 Debt
Tranche 2		
Tranche 3		

FUNDS FLOW

FUNDS FLOW	JUN 13	JUN 14	JUN 15	JUN 16	JUN 17
Profit before.Tax	261	303	318	559	768
Depreciation	18	96	31	43	55
Corporation Tax Paid	(35)	(17)	(96)	(47)	(116)
Capex	(89)	(760)	(60)	(60)	(60)
Share Capital Raised	–	–	–	–	–
(Increase) in Debtors	(13)	(3)	(7)	(9)	(11)
(Increase) in Stock	–	–	–	–	–
(Increase) in Other Debtors	(105)	(51)	(20)	(30)	(3)
Increase in Current Liabilities	22	453	22	11	24
Movement in cash	59	22	187	468	656
Movement against budget		(193)	(94)	(232)	(347)
Closing Cash	**152**	**174**	**361**	**829**	**1,485**

Sales, profits and cashflow are all summarised on one page, and historic and future results are displayed so that their relationship can be demonstrated and you and your lenders can assess if they are reasonable. If you are looking to borrow, this will potentially show lenders why you need their money, but it may even show you that you don't need as much as you thought. I have seen a borrowing requirement of

£2 million reduced to £200,000 just by a detailed analysis of the way the business worked and a careful set of predictions about how its cash would actually flow.

There has never been any shortage of institutions and individuals who are willing to lend to growing businesses that know how much they want and what the terms of business must be in order to secure it. Today's challenger banks and the new peer-to-peer lenders have increased the choice of possible funding sources, but the principal terms are unchanged:

1. The company will probably have to pledge some or all of its assets as security for the funds being borrowed.

2. If the funding is asset based (usually plant, equipment, vehicles or debtors, but occasionally stock), that may be all the security required.

3. If the borrower appears risky to the lender, due to a short period of trading (less than three years) or because there is not enough security in the business to cover the loan, personal guarantees may be demanded too. Using your own personal assets to guarantee that the company will repay its debts is a serious undertaking, but it's an acceptable risk that shouldn't alarm you, if you observe the following rules.

   a. Only guarantee your share (if you are a 60% shareholder, guarantee 60% of the loan).

   b. Don't mortgage your home. If it's co-owned, this shouldn't be required.

   c. Keep the forecasts up to date and check that they show, based on realistic assumptions, that the company can pay the money back.

It's important to raise any money you're going to need when things are going well, not when they're going badly. When people remark that a banker is someone who will lend you an umbrella when it's sunny and take it away when it's raining, they are being slightly unfair in that banks aren't that quick to snatch their umbrellas away (as I'll explain later). But no-one will lend money to a company that's making losses, except as part of a deal to more or less take the company over from the current owners. So make sure that you borrow money when things look good, when there are profits to be seen and you can show some growth or a credible plan to achieve it.

If you start making losses, it's unlikely that you will lose the business, because the lender has built in contingency to allow this to happen, by only advancing an amount that's less than the full value of the security you have

> Make sure you borrow money when things look good

pledged. Fundamentally, lenders are like any other business, looking to have happy customers who want to come back for more as they expand. Even though this may not happen all the time, they will still support you if you maintain up-to-date and realistic information, acknowledge any problems that arise and explain the action you are taking to deal with them.

If the outlook shows continual negative cashflow until the money runs out, or only looks positive on unrealistic assumptions (such as a bumper month in August, when the company usually performs best at Christmas), get professional help from an insolvency practitioner. The specialist's involvement will reassure your lenders that you are behaving properly (since lenders often rely on them themselves) and will provide advice that will enable you to stop trading before the assets available in the company to cover the loan disappear. Even if there is a shortfall, this can be repaid over time or negotiated down to a compromise figure that will allow a swift resolution and enable both parties to move on. You may also be able to go into administration, a legal process that can allow you to carry on trading without risking your personal assets.

Professionally handled, lenders are unlikely to arrive at a position where they will pursue you for every penny and sell your home out from under you. But you must keep them informed. If you continue to make losses, don't understand why, don't tell anyone the reasons and don't have a credible solution to propose, they will quite rightly begin to panic. They won't advance any more money and will start looking at how they can recover what's owed to them.

I haven't mentioned interest rates or costs yet. That's because they're not as important as people tend to think. The rate for each type of loan is fairly standard and the amount of interest you pay is rarely a significant cost in the profit and loss account. The main aim, when managing cashflow, is to be able to trade without worrying whether you have enough cash to survive and achieve your ambitions.

Problems

Many self-help books set out the steps they are recommending you to take as if they are perfectly achievable by everyone all the time. If we fail to follow these books as avidly as we might, it's because we know that life isn't like that, and they offer few hints about what to do if things go wrong.

We want suggestions for a Plan B, and they don't show us any. Some problems are technical; you don't need me to tell you how to fix those. But where you're not getting a good return from your resources of people, time and money, I can offer you five Plan Bs. Each of them specifically addresses one of the problems you may be facing:

1. Lost sales and margins.

2. Performance issues.

3. Organisational issues.

4. Contractual issues.

5. Being so stuck that you just don't know what to do.

None of these solutions will be any good until you've accepted that there's something wrong. The natural reaction to a problem is to deny it, first of all, because problems represent danger and our instinct is to avoid it. Jim Collins, in *Good to Great*, says you should 'confront the brutal facts, yet never lose faith'. So the first thing you need to do is acknowledge that there's a problem and try to define exactly what it is. Analytical skills are useful here.

Lost sales and margins

Many how-to books in this area assume that sales and profits go up and up and never turn down, even for brief periods (indeed, my illustrations are also guilty of this). But, as we all know, it doesn't always work out like that. Market conditions change, new competitors emerge and good customer relationships go into a decline when your contact moves on or up. There are three things to do to address the loss of sales and margins:

> ▶ **Attend to the customers.** Standards almost inevitably slip over time. Inertia and the reasonable nature of many customers mean that sales don't drop off straight away, as soon as standards start to fall. But at some stage there may be a significant number who feel your standards are unacceptable and move on – or refuse to pay their bills and then move on. Don't squirm around trying to find ways of persuading them the service is actually acceptable. Even if you have statistics on your side, it's their perception that counts. Ask them why it's no longer all right, and, when you have gathered the evidence, act on what they say. It's probably unnecessary to deal with 'nice to have' grumbles and you should also be wary of those who simply say that it's expensive, unless you have recently upped your prices. Find the specific areas of failure that need to be addressed, such as delivery times and quality (making sure that it's good), tell the dissatisfied customers that they are going to be fixed, and when, and just get on with it. Let all your customers know of the improvements you're making.

▸ **Add new products.** There is a finite market for everything and satisfied customers with good products are often happy to just leave it at that, without necessarily coming back to you for more. They will be tempted to add new things from wherever they find them. So be those new things. We'll look at this in more detail later (see Realistic Numbers, p.183).

▸ **Reduce costs.** If competing products are being offered at lower prices, you will need to cut your price and accept lower margins or innovate simply to maintain sales volume. You may feel forced to source items overseas, to match your competitors' low costs. Or you may decide to tough it out, hold on to your UK supplier and hope that the competitor quickly runs into the quality and delivery problems that are always likely to occur when sourcing from the other side of the world. Either strategy can be right, and only time will tell. The only guidance I can give you is to be aware that you still have a choice. You don't have to follow the pack, until that particular course emerges as clearly correct. Delay can be costly, of course, but doing some careful research before acting will lessen the risk and make your decision a better one.

> In a perfect world, people would
> perform as you expect, all the time

Performance issues

The most common problem you'll come across is performance. In a perfect world, people would perform as you expect, all the time. The truth is, though, that they won't, because we are all imperfect. But it's also helpful to recognise that generally we are all trying to do the best we can, in the circumstances we find ourselves in, and that people's failings are not deliberate.

So if the credit controller didn't call Maybepay Ltd on Friday because their balance was at the bottom of the report and she missed it when the printer had a wobbly, don't blame her for the fact that they went into administration on Monday.

In 2014, I sailed around the UK. I'd heard a friend of mine characterise this kind of coastal sailing as 'moving from one disaster to the next', so I was quietly pleased that after 47 days at sea I had dodged every storm and steered clear of the trawlers (the lorry drivers of the sea) and countless lobster pots to get within 20 miles of Ipswich, my final destination, without any mishaps at all. But, of course, as soon as I started to relax, things went haywire. I'd been checking the tides religiously throughout the voyage, but I took my eye off the ball that night. Having celebrated the achievement with my ever-reliable companion, Harvey, in the warm autumn sunshine overlooking the gorgeous River Deben the night before, I woke up in a pea-souper, cautiously got under way – and promptly had a close encounter with the river bank, though to this day I can't tell you whether it was the right or left one.

Nor is it usually the case that mistakes happen early on, either in the company or in the period of employment. They generally occur later, when overconfidence sets in.

If you observe repeated failings, you may find yourself getting annoyed and saying, or wanting to say, things like 'You never turn up on time.' You should recognise that this is an emotional response, rather than a rational one. In this annoyed, frustrated state, we tend to generalise, distort or delete, making sweeping negative statements and ignoring any positives. Acting while you're feeling like this won't help solve the problem, because, as discussed before, when you push me, I push back. This pushing back is instinctive, and there is no resolution, just continual pushing against each other. Instead, I advocate following the formula set out by Susan Scott in her influential book, *Fierce Conversations: Achieving Success in Work and in Life, One Conversation at a Time*. The natural reaction, when we are upset, is to list all the things that have upset us and expect the other person to see immediately that those things are wrong. Scott suggests that you do it differently and follow these six steps, which I have illustrated:

1. State objectively and specifically what your issue is: *'Can we discuss your timekeeping, please?'*

2. Explain why the issue is significant to you. It's rarely the case that we understand why the other person is upset. Explaining this reduces the other person's fear about having done wrong and makes that person feel less defensive and more able to accept what you are saying. *'It's important, because you are a front-of-house staff member, that you are on time. Otherwise colleagues are forced to cover for you, and that's not fair on them.'*

3. Set out your ideal outcome. This shows the possible endpoint, a proposal to be discussed, which means the conversation can be directed to a goal (a win-win position), rather than being about winning or losing an argument. *'I'd like you to turn up on time.'*

4. Set out, accurately, the relevant background information. Only after the first three steps do you bring forward the actions, behaviour or statements that have created the issue. Now that the issue is clear and an outcome has been presented, it is possible to review these matters with less guilt, anxiety, fear or anger. *'According to the records in the office, you have been 20 minutes late or more three times in the last week.'*

5. Explain your actions and thoughts to date. No situation is ever entirely one person's responsibility. Demonstrating that you have thought about the situation and made some effort to move towards a resolution shows that you are not here to dump all the blame and responsibility for a solution on the other person. *'I'm wondering if you're OK. Would you like to take some time off?'*

6. Set out the help you would like from the other person. Explain specifically what it is that that person could do for you. *'Perhaps you'd like to tell me what has caused this, so that we can find a solution?'*

This should ideally be done as one statement, after which you should be prepared to listen to the other person's point of view. You will usually find there's an explanation that shows the person did what seemed to be best in a difficult situation. *'My baby sometimes screams when the new child-minder arrives, and I need to soothe her before I can leave.'* Then you can work together to find a solution, such as asking the child-minder to arrive earlier, replacing her or rearranging shift times for a month and then reviewing the situation.

After this, if there is no improvement, you can ask the employee to leave, giving the notice stipulated in the employment contract. The decision to dismiss an employee often causes great anxiety among employers, as there is a general belief that UK employment law is loaded in favour of the employee and that, if you say anything at all, you will be sued for compensation of £50,000 or more. This isn't quite true. What I believe the law requires is that the employer should be grown-up and emotionally intelligent and not react emotionally to something that upsets him or her. By following Scott's method, you will have discussed the situation and attempted to resolve it. If there is no significant change, you are then entitled to take further steps:

- ▸ If the issue is a failure to learn the skills the role entails, you can reassign the employee, but you don't have to.

- ▸ If it's an attitude problem, I suggest that you ask (leading with questions) if the person is happy in the job. I have parted company with a few capable people who were just not right for my business by asking if they felt this was the right company for them.

- ▸ You can follow up with verbal and written warnings, which explain, rationally, what the issue is and what needs to be done to rectify it.

If you're still unsure about how to handle these matters, employ an HR specialist who has done it all before. Make sure that this person has experience of handling these situations with skill and empathy and is not just following a legal process, because that could lead to the case coming to court, since that is where legal processes end up.

Organisational issues

It's natural to expect to be able to grow by repeating what has worked well in the past. But growing a business will require you, at certain points, to break the pattern and change the way things are done. You should be encouraged, rather than alarmed, if there is a significant amount of staff turnover as the business starts to expand and the workforce moves from a handful to a larger team of 10 people or more. People who joined in the early days move on because 'It's not like it used to be', and because the way of working changes from everyone piling in together to a more structured approach based on organisation, vision and values. At this new stage of the development of the business, you need a new type of person, one who will operate within a structure, rather than being happy to work in the midst of organised chaos.

> Growing a business will require you, at certain points, to break the pattern and change the way things are done

Not all the old guard will leave, and the overall result should be a good blend of different skills and personality types:

- ▸ Those who have been with you a while and have taken some ownership of the systems so that they run smoothly and can adapt to changing circumstances.

- ▸ Newcomers who can look at the business with fresh eyes and suggest innovations that would not occur to those who are familiar with the way things have been done up to now.

Contractual issues

As well as employment agreements and organisational understandings, your business is created by a web of contracts with outsiders. Sometimes these contracts no longer work well, due to a change in circumstances, such as a takeover. Sometimes one of the parties is trying to gain an advantage – maybe a customer or supplier wanting a better price from you. Rather than saying yes or no, imagine the solution as one corner of an isosceles triangle:

The customer or supplier's position is one base corner, your position is the other base corner and the solution is at the top – not between you, but somewhere else. Don't just look at the bare facts of each position, but look around and see what else could work. What could the customer or supplier be given that could also be of some benefit to you? It's amazing how often this approach turns tempers from bad to good and snarls into smiles. The answer may be a different product for less money, seasonal discounts, a faster delivery schedule for a small premium or new packaging to fit on the shelves better. All of these changes might fit neatly into this win-win category, and there are many other situations where creative thinking can produce mutually beneficial results, not just with customers and suppliers, but with everyone you deal with.

If there is no satisfactory resolution after trying this, you can still say no. No matter how essential the other person's involvement appears to be, there will be a point at which it really isn't worth carrying on doing business together (for example, selling to a retailer at cost, as mentioned in Expanding Sales, p.138). If you can't find a solution yourself, it makes sense to seek advice, though it's important to make sure that the person who advises you adopts the same win-win approach to problem-solving. In my experience, if there is a dispute, people usually turn to their lawyers for advice. I've done it myself. The advice you get may be that your opponent is right, or at least has a strong case. If we don't like what we're hearing, we often reject this counsel in favour of 'the right advice', and that is usually a mistake. Even if you feel that you are absolutely right, be very careful, even if the other side has already gone legal.

Once you have started legal proceedings, costs can rise rapidly. The financing of disputes is changing, and 'no win, no fee' arrangements are now available for some types of action. But it is still the norm for most cases to be run on the basis of an hourly rate for the lawyers, because of the impossibility of predicting costs with any certainty. It is hard to oppose such a stance, but once both sides adopt it, the legal costs will mount very fast:

> ▶ I have seen one patent infringement action where both barristers stated that they didn't know why the case had come to court. The answer was, at least partly, the £1.4 million in legal fees that was paid by one side.

> ▶ I was originally quoted an estimated £75,000 to defend a claim against my family company for £400,000. By the time the case had wound its way through the legal process, the upshot was a settlement in the sum of £90,000 – and legal fees totalling roughly £400,000.

There is also a little-known product called after-the-event insurance, a counterintuitive type of insurance policy that funds litigation for something that has *already* gone wrong. It's not universally available and it's not cheap. But if you have a good case and the other side is refusing to co-operate primarily because it is thought that you can't afford to litigate, it can be highly effective.

It's easy to get stuck on one outcome and to fight for it. The energy we get from the feeling that we have been treated unfairly is strong and rooted deep in our psyche. But it's not helpful to you if you desire WealthBeing. It detracts from the resources that are available to put into the business and the chances

Have the courage to say sorry even if you feel it is unjustified

of getting the result you are aiming for are very small indeed. Even slam-dunk legal cases often have a sting in the tail of unrecoverable costs – and the bad feeling of the loser is of no benefit to you.

Don't lose sight of the fact that the problem will eventually have to be resolved, one way or another. Use arbitration or mediation to help find a workable solution. Have the courage to meet the other person and say sorry, even if you feel it is unjustified. Why? Because it works for you. Find the top of the isosceles triangle, using like-minded advisers, and the problem will go away, leaving you free to get on with your life.

Being stuck

In the worst case, your business may find itself in a situation that seems hopeless. You've done everything right, resolving employee conflicts, re-engineering the product and solving the cashflow issues, but you are still not growing. In fact, your records show that sales are down for each of the last six months.

If you are facing a situation like this, first try two simple steps:

1. Look through the fingers. Imagine I am holding my hand up in front of your face. What do you see? My fingers. But if you adjust your focus you can look through my fingers and see my face. It's the same with problems. Look beyond the immediate issues and see what else you can see.

After we had had a couple of successful years in an exclusive alliance relationship with accountants BDO, the firm announced that it was dismantling all its alliances. This decision was triggered by new guidelines from the Institute of Chartered Accountants in England and Wales that required auditors to not just be independent but be seen to be independent. The new rules meant that BDO couldn't be in an alliance with us any more. At first sight, this looked like causing a serious drop in future referrals. But when we looked beyond this, we saw that it gave us a new opportunity to market ourselves to other accounting firms. BDO is now just one of many referrers sending business our way.

2.   Go away. Problems look less daunting when viewed from a distance. If you can't get that distance in your mind, because the situation seems so grave, go somewhere else to discuss it.

Gordon Durham & Co lost an opportunity for a new partnership in September 2006, a few weeks before the directors were about to take a break in New York. We felt initially that we should cancel our trip, since to be seen to flee from the problem and go on an expensive trip would not go down well with our colleagues. But we recalled how successful other similar trips had been and realised that our position was not bad. It was just not as good as it might have been. So we went ahead. We came back with a fresh perspective and the feeling that this loss was just a blip. We had also, it seems, acquired a new determination that enabled us to seize other opportunities as they arose over the next few months.

If these tips don't work, if you feel well and truly stuck, trapped in your current ways of thinking and unable to see a way out, try asking yourself these ten questions. If you can answer them, you can change everything:

1.   In relation to your problem, what are the three main barriers to progress?

2.   Of these three, what is the one that, if changed, would alter everything?

3.   Just for now, imagine that you could change anything you wanted. How would this one thing have to change to move your problem closer to resolution?

4.   When you imagine that you have made these changes, how does it feel?

5. What, specifically, stops this from happening?

6. What would you have to do, or stop doing, to overcome this hurdle?

7. What stops you?

8. If you knew what to do differently, could you do it?

9. If you knew you could do it, would you?

10. When?

These are difficult questions. I have sometimes failed to answer even the first one. But if you persevere, you'll find they provide a useful, practical tool to help get you out of a place where everything seems hopeless.

WealthBeing check

Wealth

Having expanded sales and built a team that you have learnt to lead, you will now have a business that could look something like this:

PROFIT AND LOSS ACCOUNTS

Activity	Item	£'000	Comments
	Sales	1,600.0	
	Cost of Sales	-885.0	Including bad debts of, say, 2.5%
Gross profit		**715.0**	
Staff	Admin, Service, Sales & Marketing People	-350.0	
Marketing	Travel & Subsistence	-35.0	
	Website	-25.0	
Premises	Office	-55.0	
IT/Comms	IT	-20.0	
	Phones & Internet	-25.0	
Admin	Insurance	-15.0	
	Financial Control	-40.0	
	Sundries	-5.0	
Profit/(loss)		**145.0**	
	Tax	-29.0	
	Dividend to You	-40.0	
Retained in the Business		**76.0**	

The balance sheet now looks like this:

BALANCE SHEETS

Item	£'000	Comments
Fixed Assets	.0	
Debtors	280.0	Sales are more regular so debtors are 45-60 days sales
Creditors	-154.0	There are some large creditors and debts that will have to be paid, especially Corporation Tax
Working Capital	126.0	Still important but manageable, so long as you forecast when the major payments are due
Cash at Bank	-28.2	You'll need a facility of £50,000 to cover short-term fluctuations
Loan From You		You'll need to capitalise the loan balance to support borrowings
Net Assets	97.8	
Share Capital	30.6	Including capitalising the remainder of your loan
P&L Account	67.2	
Net Worth	97.8	

As I said in the Introduction, growth rarely goes in a straight line, with the same percentage growth each year. Usually the rate of growth increases year by year, so the start seems slow and then suddenly things seem to happen much more quickly. It often takes three or more years to get to this stage, with at least half the growth coming in the last year. As sales pass £1 million, you have reached an important milestone, because you have now created something that is recognisable as an organisation. Your income will now be increasing, at long last, beyond the salary you used to earn.

Wellbeing

Here's that WealthBeing graph again, updated to reflect the progress you've made.

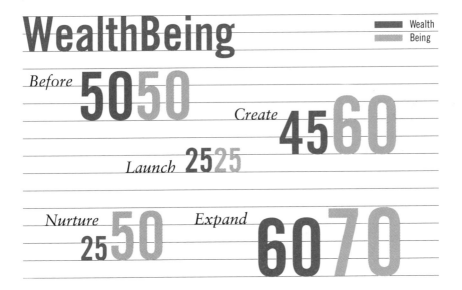

There is a lot to learn, as your business grows. Developing the new skills you need and seeing the successes that have flowed from your idea and are now multiplying fast can go a long way towards satisfying your need to achieve something significant. But challenges don't always turn into victories, and you will feel any losses personally. To maintain your sense of wellbeing, I suggest you learn to look at the business in a slightly different way:

▸ Observe the percentages: if you are getting 70% of things right, you are succeeding. If it's 80%, you are exceptional. If it looks like 90%, you may not be going as far as you could. Have confidence in yourself, remember what Samuel Beckett said ('Fail again. Fail better'), and accept that failing sometimes is a good thing.

▸ Know where the business ends and you start. Whether you leave its problems at the office or learn to compartmentalise your life more, you must find ways to switch off from the business and stop it controlling you.

▸ You can choose whether or not to be upset by a failure.

One of my colleagues claims he visualises a metaphorical baseball bat and uses it to beat problems away when he knows there's a danger that they will get him down. Another, otherwise normal, friend imagines himself putting on chainmail armour, under his clothes, as he gets ready to catch the 7.13 in the mornings.

▸ Learn where and how to share. I have mentioned the growing aura of power and authority that will stop you being one of the lads, and this can make you feel lonely. Your life partner can provide comfort but won't be able to provide solutions, unless he or she is also in business. There are several organisations dedicated to providing useful support in these circumstances, connecting people with similar problems who can share their experiences, feelings and solutions. The best I've come across are the recently formed ABLE (Academy for Business Leaders and Entrepreneurs), Vistage (which has been around since the 1950s), the Academy for Chief Executives and the Supper Club, of which I'm a member.

▸ Take care of yourself. Continue to take regular breaks, exercise and eat well. Above all, use the techniques of meditation to stay relaxed and manage your emotions. Observe when you are getting angry or upset, look for the cause, (use the Negative Information and Negative Feeling tools) and deal with it. If you've managed to keep up some meditation or mindfulness practice, you may have started to appreciate that feelings of worry and anxiety are part of the human condition, an experience you share with the rest of us. Becoming aware of this will help to fortify you considerably and remind you that this, too, shall pass.

As you become more experienced, you will face fewer problems. You will be able to see what is important before it becomes urgent and get the right people doing the right things.

Developing new skills can go a long way to satisfying your need to achieve something significant

6

BUILDING AND SELLING IT

Introduction

It may strike you as a little odd that, as soon as you have a business that is turning over £1 million+ with a £100,000 profit, I am insisting on turning your attention to the subject of selling it. There are two good reasons, however, why you should think about selling your creation as soon as it is recognisable as a business:

1.   Your limitations.

2.   The business's limitations.

Let's look at these before setting out how to approach making it saleable, working out how much you need and getting the right price.

Your limitations

You will surely enjoy creating and running the enterprise, and be rewarded for your efforts in both material and emotional ways. But not all the time. As the business expands, the number and complexity of the challenges rises. Knowing how to win, creativity, endurance and having the emotional intelligence to cope with other people will remain essential assets. But there will still be situations where you are pushed to your limits. This guide will enable you to cope with most of these most of the time, but at some stage you will run out of capacity to deal with them all. Why? For the simple reason that it happens to everyone.

When you find yourself in this situation, you will be faced with a choice – change yourself, or change your position.

- ▸ If wealth is your overriding aim, you will change yourself. In my opinion there is a point in every business at which further wealth creation becomes a challenge to the moral compass of the leaders. It's not a question of size but of growth and how it's achieved. To put it simply - if growth is determined exclusively by spreadsheets and financial statements which trumps wellbeing in every discussion, the business is focussed solely on wealth creation. If the business is moving in this direction then pay attention to this. If you feel that you're being pushed beyond your capacity to deal with the problems in ways that feel good, the only way to cope is by erecting whatever defences you can to stop them damaging your health and soldiering on (an apt word, if ever there was one). These defences make you more distant from the world and there is an added disbenefit in that they reduce your ability to be connected – to lead others – because you are now significantly different from them. You may even find yourself controlling and even manipulating them through the power that wealth gives you, but that, in my opinion, is not WealthBeing.

- ▸ If WealthBeing is truly your aim, you will change your position. WealthBeing acknowledges that you need a balance between wealth and wellbeing. That will be achieved through selling the business, well before it becomes spreadsheet driven, to give you enough secure, accessible wealth, increasing your wellbeing by meeting the higher needs set out by Maslow's Hierarchy of Needs, and still being connected to others (Maslow's third Need). That connection is still there because, while people respect your ability, you haven't lost your humility and the sense of awe and wonderment that you have achieved this.

You also face a more basic limitation – this mortal coil. You aren't immortal, and as long as you are one of the driving forces in the business, it will wither and die when you do. You could bring in younger people as junior partners or minority shareholders and you could recruit your children into the business. Many people do. But in my opinion there are more downsides to this than upsides:

1. The ownership structure becomes complicated and the views of different generations, with different time horizons and different desires, make it hard to agree on the direction the business should take.

2. The business needs to survive for many years – 20 or 30, perhaps – and markets change significantly, sometimes every two or three years, so there is added uncertainty.

3. Unless the success of the business has been so great that you have enough wealth outside it to thrive, your fortune is still tied up in the business and is dependent on a small number of people.

Duncan Cheatle, founder of the Supper Club, one of the best networks of business owners, supports my belief that finally separating yourself from the business is almost always a last essential step. Holding on too long, perhaps in the hope of getting the perfect deal, is a temptation that Duncan feels business owners need to resist. He's seen it happen too often. 'In my experience, more entrepreneurs regret not selling than regret the price they got when they sold,' he says.

The business's limitations

Whatever business you have created, it must eventually die. Even though you will have become competent in business and have brought together a team with all the necessary functional competencies, every idea eventually becomes at least partially redundant, overtaken by the next innovation. Who would have thought, for example, in 2005, that those all-powerful BlackBerries and Nokia phones would no longer be the worldwide business tools of choice in ten years' time? If you wait until this is clear, you will have lost the opportunity to benefit from what you have created, and maybe to create something else. Even established serial entrepreneurs keep moving on. Sir Richard Branson is involved in space tourism, railways, aviation, mobile phones and healthcare, among many other industries, but he's no longer in the record business.

Change is ever present and the pace of change continues to increase. Its effects may not be as dramatic as being made obsolete by a new product, but a series of smaller issues outside your control can put a stop to growth. Senior people can have mid-life crises and leave, maybe to join your competitors. Valued customers will have re-organisations and change their policies, leaving you out in the cold, and exciting new markets become less profitable with the arrival of cheap imitations and onerous regulations.

The approach to building and selling it

When you're selling a business, you need to think of it not as a source of income but as an asset, because people buy and sell assets, not incomes. The difference may seem like a matter of semantics, but it's not. If you're buying an asset, it needs to be discrete, separate from its owners. Like any other asset, it needs to be in good condition. It also needs to be something that potential purchasers can take away and use the way they want to use it. How many perfectly good kitchens have you seen ripped out by the new owners because they just didn't like them? Some of the things purchasers do to newly acquired businesses may look just as brutal as that to the sellers. But it's only when you can accept the buyer's right to do this that you have got yourself in the right position to sell. To get there, I suggest you start by admitting that you have a sentimental attachment to your business. Enjoy this feeling and then start letting it go. You will need to have moved beyond this kind of emotional tie by the time you are ready to sell.

This chapter sets out your next steps under three major headings:

1. Making the business saleable.

2. Working out how much money you need.

3. Getting that sum.

> Change is ever present and the pace of change continues to increase

Making the business saleable

In order for a business to be one that another company will buy, it needs three things:

► Its own unique, or nearly unique, **place in the world.**

► **Independent management and robust processes.**

► **Realistic numbers** – profits, prices and margins, and everything that drives them.

Its place in the world

Until 2001, my family company, Gordon Durham & Co, was a jobbing builder, like many other building firms. It won contracts simply by tendering the lowest price. Because it wasn't unique, it struggled to make a profit in this highly competitive market. And it had no value.

In 2001, the business model changed. Sir John Egan, the former chief executive of Jaguar, issued a report that revolutionised the way all government bodies, including councils, government-subsidised housing associations *et al*, procured their buildings. Whereas competitive tendering seemed to be the cheapest way of funding development projects, Sir John pointed out that it wasn't, because costs often increased during construction as builders sought to boost their profits by re-pricing contracts whenever specifications changed. Egan said the whole supply chain, from materials producers to end users, should work together, as companies did in the automotive industry, to achieve lower overall costs. Re-pricing could be largely eliminated, as designs could be discussed before they were issued. To make this revolutionary approach work, councils and housing associations should not issue tenders, but form business partnerships with selected building contractors, who would get a steady stream of work but would be expected to use their skills to reduce overall costs.

The effect of this change on the Gordon Durham & Co business was huge. Instead of being an opportunistic jobbing builder, it could now form long-term partnerships with its customers – alongside others, as most councils chose to work with two or three partners – within which it could add value and generate profits. Gordon Durham & Co soon found it had a nearly unique place in the world, as one of the partners of North Tyneside Council and various other bodies. It was these relationships that turned the company into a saleable asset.

Gordon Durham & Co wasn't the only contractor to gain from the post-Egan arrangements. Some of our competitors were also benefiting to some extent, though many others failed to form these new business partnerships and struggled to survive.

Assess your place in the world by comparison with your competitors. Keep an eye on them and see how they measure up:

- ▸ See what their accounts show: are they profitable? Do they have cash in the bank?

- ▸ See what they are selling.

- ▸ See how they price things: are prices all-inclusive? When do they charge premiums?

- ▸ Ask your customers how they rate them, without doing their promotional work for them.

Don't go thinking your competitors are miles better than you. They haven't won everything, have they? Even if they are much bigger than you and have some top people working for them, they are still staffed by human beings. They may have some better systems than you, but they will probably have some legacy issues, too, that restrict their

> Don't go thinking your competitors are miles better than you

flexibility – things like, for example, an inability to make new package deals available to existing customers as well as new buyers. They may also have managers dealing with day-to-day issues who don't have the discretion or initiative to satisfy a particular customer's needs in the way an owner-managed business like yours can.

Keep your eyes open and your ear to the ground, so that you become aware of what is unique to you and what makes people choose you ahead of your competitors – and vice versa. As with selling products, it's easy to fall into the trap of looking at features rather than benefits. One of the features of the Beneteau yachts' new 'Dock & Go' feature is that you can turn the propeller 90 degrees. The benefit is that it's much easier to moor it in a crowded marina, without providing free entertainment for passers-by.

By establishing relationships with larger customers and developing significant points of difference in how you do things that others can't replicate, at a comparable price, you can nurture the aspects of the business that make it saleable.

Independent management and robust processes

Children grow up, learn to look after themselves and move out of your home. If your children weren't independent, they couldn't leave, and the same applies to businesses. Once they have demonstrated their independence, they are able to go their own way. So it is important to be able to demonstrate that the business can exist independently, without your involvement. This makes it saleable, because it can then be separated from you without losing its value.

The main essentials for this are independent management and robust processes. We have looked at the basics of management, culture and processes already, but this is the time to do three things:

1. Set standards.

2. Fix clear structures.

3. Further shape people's behaviours.

Standards can now be spelt out so that everyone in the business understands just what is required. The first standard is adherence to the strategy. The primary role of the leader, whether or not it is you, is to make sure the strategy is explained to everyone, and, equally importantly, that everyone has the opportunity to feed back how it plays out in practice. That may lead to alterations, but everyone must be clear that the strategy can only be changed when the board of directors changes it. Until then, individuals are expected to perform to the best of their ability in carrying it out. Use the market intelligence you have gathered and make sure you achieve at least the same levels as your competitors in terms of response times and service levels. Be true to the values of the business by ensuring that teamwork, in which everyone gives their own skills to help others move the action, team or organisation forward, is standard behaviour. Be clear what success looks like and allow all the information

> It is important to be able to demonstrate that the business can exist independently, without your involvement

that is needed to be shared. Don't hold it back because it's confidential; hold it back if there's a good reason – because it's confusing or simply not helpful. Allocated overheads sent down from on high and details of individual salaries should both be held back, but how the unit's profit is arrived at should be carefully explained.

Dynamic, newish businesses with new products that excite people don't adapt easily to the demands of a more structured approach. Indeed, some of your people may have joined you precisely because of what they saw as rigid and oppressive structures at their previous jobs. So be aware of this and keep your structure minimalist, with as few embellishments as possible. It's essential that the board gives a clear direction, each business unit knows what it exists to do, and support functions don't become autonomous and just satisfy themselves with 'doing what it says on the tin' (in this case, support).

You should have created an infrastructure that is fit for purpose, but it's helpful to review it frequently so that it still works well. If no-one keeps an eye out for this sort of thing, there will be at least one person who spends four hours or more every week transferring information from one system to another with a cheerful cry of 'It doesn't matter – it doesn't take me long.'

Jobs should be clearly defined, so that performance can be measured. In young companies, the directors often see the firm's growth itself as a sign of progress. But individuals further down the organisation don't see their progress as being so directly tied to that of the company, unless it's shown to them.

With a structure such as this, you can work on the last, most difficult aspect, which is behaviour. Everyone agrees these days that good behaviour needs to be modelled by the leaders, so I shall set out how directors should act, on the understanding that others are expected to follow these rules wherever appropriate. The clearest way to explain this is by looking at behaviour before, during and after board meetings.

1. Directors should trust each other. I set out the trust equation in Chapter 3 – Credibility, Reliability and Intimacy, divided by

Self-orientation – and it's applicable to each director. Make sure that people can do their jobs, on time, are personable and are not just in it for themselves. Underscore these points by insisting that they talk straight, to the point, restraining their emotions and leaving their personal agendas outside.

2. There is a risk that board meetings are accepted as being about nothing more than a minute dissection of the latest accounts, interspersed with almost random contributions from people who think they have just had their views validated and believe the company will now move in the direction they always thought it should. I've seen this myself, far too often. Since each participant in this scenario goes away with this view, the chances of it being true are actually zero. There are also likely to be some board members who are obsessed with strategy and fail to relate it to current realities.

There are a handful of golden rules that will make any board an effective decision-making body:

▸   Look at both micro and macro issues, and ensure that they connect. If people are on top of their functions and understand the aims of the business, this is not as difficult as it sounds.

▸   Time is a scarce resource and should always be used well, and board meetings take up a significant amount of time for the organisation's best people. So issue the agenda and papers three working days in advance and make sure directors don't waste their time looking over the results together in the meeting. The papers should encapsulate performance to date in each function (sales, marketing, production, HR, finance and IT) and a forecast, based on results to date, that covers the rest of the financial year and, ideally, 12 months into the future. Make sure these reports are short, as that will force people to put some thought into their preparation. And be careful not to assume that the business will revert to performing in line with the budget if actual results are below that level. Make sure that balance sheet assumptions reflect reality, too. If there is a slowdown in customer collections, or a significant bad debt, that must be reflected in the numbers.

▶ The agenda should ensure that past, present and future issues are discussed, with enough background information to support informed debate. A typical agenda might look like this:

Formalities	Approve last month's minutes as a true record (only discuss matters not dealt with elsewhere in the agenda, or the meeting will lose its structure).
Past	Comparison of results with forecast and budget. Any surprises? Look at the balance sheet, as well as the P&L.
Present	▪ Where are sales coming from? Is this in line with expectations? Are volumes where they should be? What other feedback are we getting from customers? ▪ Is quality good? ▪ How are people performing? ▪ Is the infrastructure still fit for purpose?
Future	▪ What products are we developing and what can we develop? ▪ How can we market ourselves? ▪ What are our competitors doing?
Any other business	This is often where the really difficult issues appear, so avoid the tendency to pack papers away before it has been dealt with.

Fix the time to be spent on each item and ensure that this is adhered to. If you're often taking longer, it's likely that people are repeating the same points and not listening to each other. Don't confuse polite listening with generous listening.

In an engaged company with enthusiastic directors, there is ample opportunity to range far and wide without concluding anything at all. Make sure that difficult issues are raised and discussed. At the end of each section, and at the end of the meeting, the chairman should summarise the decisions that have been reached, so that these can be minuted (minuting all the discussions, rather than just the conclusions, is of little help in SMEs).

> Mutual respect demands that I commit to implementing the decisions

3. The meeting has ended when there are decisions on each item. That's not the same as unanimous agreement, but it is as far as the rest of the company is concerned! Mutual respect demands that, even if I don't agree with you, I accept what the board says. I also recognise my responsibility as a director and commit to implementing the decision as minuted. If someone has a real problem with a decision, the only alternative is to leave the company (still keeping the decision confidential). Stated baldly, this sounds pretty tough. It can be, but the truth is that almost all decisions are acceptable to almost everyone nearly all the time. Frequent objections from one particular individual almost inevitably lead to a parting of the ways.

Bonuses and other incentives can influence behaviour, too. There are many theories about how to incentivise people and there's no guarantee that one of them will work better than the others. In choosing the right incentives for your business, I suggest the following guidelines:

1. Make sure they are understood by the recipients. If you need to show the spreadsheet on which incentives are

calculated to someone below senior management level, then it's too complicated to be an effective incentive scheme and it's not going to improve motivation. It might even dampen people's enthusiasm.

2.   Make incentives as relevant as possible to the goals of the business. If costs are fixed, use sales values as the trigger for sales staff commissions and bonuses. If the sales people have discretion over prices, then award incentives based on gross profit, or have stepped percentages based on the price achieved (which a good accountant can work out for you).

3.   Ensure there's a win-win, making sure the company is better off, too. This sounds obvious and easily achievable, but you may want to pay override commissions (such as payments to those who manage the salesman who gets the initial bonus), as well as normal incentives.

4.   Never, ever go back on what you have agreed. Backtracking demoralises people and can create enemies within the firm. If there is a grey area, be careful to explain your interpretation and get it agreed. Even this has its risks, but fortunately it should seldom be necessary.

5.   If you are thinking of issuing bonuses in the form of shares, you will run into another level of complexity. Tax concessions make share bonuses attractive, from the company's point of view, but don't allow this to affect your decision. You need to know that recipients both want the shares and understand how they work. Many a well-intentioned boss has made a generous award of shares, only to discover that people see this as being paid in funny money. Share bonuses can be expensive and troublesome, too, unless you apply three more rules:

   a. Award them only when performance targets have been reached.

b. Make sure these shares can be sold to the purchaser when the business is acquired.

c. Make sure the company can buy the shares back if the employee leaves. You'll need valuations of the company for this, as well as for the issue. For awards of a few shares – or even for 20% – the value of the company can be taken as being roughly three times its profit before tax for the last financial year, because the small size of the shareholding makes it less valuable than a larger one in the eyes of HMRC.

Finally you need to understand who stays and who goes when the business is sold. You will have a partner or a mentor and there may be other senior people, too. It's time to have frank discussions with them about the future and about your intention to sell. This is best done as a Fierce Conversation. The gist of it could be:

- My issue is selling the business.

- It's significant because I need your co-operation.

- My ideal outcome is to get an exit for me and to give you the result you want.

- There are currently no offers on the table, but the strategy shows that we are likely to be acquired by a competitor who envies our geographical coverage.

- I know what your remuneration package is.

- I'd like to know what you'd want to do. Do you see yourself taking on a role in a larger group or would you like to exit when I do?

- A clear answer is unlikely at the first meeting, but good listening and an agreement to follow up will help you reach a mutual understanding.

In my experience, the most common reason for not selling a business is the failure to make this transfer of management authority from founders to managers. Not only does it deter buyers, who won't want to have to hire a new management team for the business after you've gone, but it can also slow down the growth of the company. Founders who can't bring themselves to make this step are usually suffering from an over-emotional attachment to the company, which gets in the way of decisions that could benefit the business. If you hear yourself vetoing suggestions with phrases like 'Over my dead body', you may still be too emotionally involved.

I realise how hard it can be to stop doing something you do for love as well as enrichment, or to let someone go who has been with you right from the start. But our aim is to achieve balance and meet all your needs. In the end, I believe you'll be glad you stepped back and left room for the development of an independent management team, as that is invariably one of the key steps towards a successful sale of the business.

Realistic numbers

You need to be able to show potential buyers that your business has enjoyed growing revenues and profits in the recent past and is likely to keep on growing in the next two to five years. The starting point for this is the key drivers, which we looked at earlier under Cashflow (see p.145). To achieve

> Our aim is to achieve balance and meet all your needs

our strategic aims, we need to revisit these drivers and work out how we can grow them. There will be a handful of key points to consider:

1. Pricing.

2. Costs.

3. Additional resources in each function.

4.   Possible new income streams.

5.   Cash to fund these.

As the business becomes established, it will be possible to increase prices beyond cost increases in the industry. People become attached to your product and are prepared to pay a bit more for it, especially if it has been refreshed or upgraded, even though these modifications are cheap to do. But there is always a limit.

The price smokeries in the UK had to pay fish farmers for their supplies of salmon shot up by 70% in 2013, with the result that many of these small, specialised businesses went bust.

For a while, it looked as if being a fish farmer and getting these high prices was an enviable situation. But as the number of smokeries decreased, demand fell and the fish farmers found their industry had a major problem of overcapacity. In 2014, the salmon price plummeted, eventually dropping back below 2012 levels.

When looking at additional resources, it's common to add new costs on top of the existing ones. A better approach is to use 'zero-based budgeting' in each area. Imagine, for instance, that you had no existing sales and marketing function. How should it look if you were only selling the new product range: some of the things that were suitable for the old range, in different market conditions, no longer produce significant results and can be stopped. As a result, the overall increase in costs will be less than you were expecting.

New income streams can be generated through selling new products or selling to new customers. This creates four options, as demonstrated by this diagram:

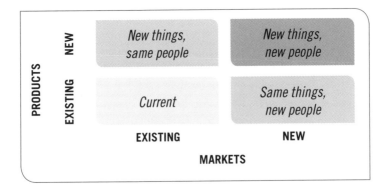

Selling new things to new people is more like setting up a new venture than developing the business. If you're going to do this, you must understand that you are effectively starting again at the beginning.

In working out the cash to fund the development of new income streams, it's common to look at the extra amount you plan to spend and then seek it from lenders or investors. But there are two problems with this:

1. It doesn't demonstrate the return to the lender or the investor, or to you.

2. It isn't the right amount.

It is far better to look at your business as an investor would, as an asset, and answer half a dozen blunt questions:

1. If we spend £x in this way, what extra profits will be generated?

2. Could that £x be funded out of profits we are already generating?

3. If not, could it be funded by borrowing against assets of ours that haven't already been used to secure loans for working capital?

4. If not, could some of it be funded by borrowing against assets that will be created (especially debtors)?

5. If not, or not entirely, do we need to find an equity investor to fund the rest?

6. If profits, after funding borrowings, are going to increase by 50%, how much of our equity could we give away without being worse off? The table below – based on the deal for an investor who is bringing in a £100,000 equity while the company borrows £100,000 – demonstrates how the sums work out:

	PRE-INVESTMENT £'000	POST-INVESTMENT £'000
Earnings before Interest & Tax ('EBIT')	100	157
Interest	0	(7)
Profit Before Tax ('PBT')	100	150
Multiplier of EBIT to Calculate Value of Shares	5	5
Value of the Enterprise, i.e. Shares + Loans	500	785
Loans to be Repaid	0	(100)
Value of Shares	500 ←	685
Value of shares of post-investment company that should be attributable to you and colleagues	└──→	500
So minimum % of equity that should be held by you and colleagues post-investment	100%	500/685 = 73%

The remaining value of the equity of £185,000 in this example would justify an investment of £100,000, generating 85% over, say, three years (a sensible time horizon at this stage). Armed with these figures, you and your advisers will be able to explain why a proposal that requires you to give away any more than 27% of the shares is not acceptable and seek the win-win. Of course, you may find an aggressive investor seeks to undermine your position and drive a hard bargain, based on the assumption that you have no other choice: 'Your company will be dead without this, because you'll fail to keep up with the competition.' But your figures have not just been plucked out of the sky, and you can show they make sense. If I came up against this kind of bullying, emotional response, I would simply find another investor. There are many, even in the range of £100,000 to £250,000 investments. And good deals for them, based on businesses with focused plans that reflect a profitable company and effective management, are still comparatively rare.

You should know, though, that relatively few companies raise equity funding for this purpose. When I surveyed a hundred companies that FD Solutions works with, I found that only just over 20% had taken investment money from outsiders.

If your expansion plans are based on more of the same, your forecast results might look something like this:

PROFIT & LOSS (£'000s)		LAST YEAR	THIS YEAR	NEXT YEAR
Sales		2,270	2,681	3,064
Gross Profit		1,352	1,633	1,840
% of Net Sales		60%	61%	60%
Expenses		1,034	1,127	1,212
Depreciation		79	55	34
Interest Received/(paid)		(1)	(3)	(6)
Profit Before Tax		**240**	**453**	**599**
Corporation Tax		(68)	(124)	(160)
Profit After Tax		171	329	439
KPIs				
Membership Growth	80%			
Net Revenue Growth		27%	18%	14%
Total Units		5,028	5,693	6,287
Unit Growth		18%	13%	10%
Units/mgr		264	273	279
Units/supervisor		984	931	883

FUNDS FLOW (£'000s)	LAST YEAR	THIS YEAR	NEXT YEAR
Net Profit/(Loss)	171	329	439
Depreciation	79	55	34
Capex	(30)	(46)	(46)
Decrease in Investments	-	68	124
Share Capital	-	-	-
(Increase) in Current Assets	(91)	(50)	(46)
Increase in Current Liabilities	172	187	165
Investments	-	-	-
Movement in Cash	301	544	670
Opening Cash	12	313	857
Cash Closing Balance	**313**	**857**	**1,528**

BALANCE SHEET (£'000s)	LAST YEAR	THIS YEAR	NEXT YEAR
Fixed Assets	**89**	**80**	**92**
Investments	**198**	**130**	**6**
Current Assets			
Debtors	313	367	417
Bad Debt Provision	(33)	(37)	(41)
Prepayments	59	59	59
Deposits & Other Assets	5	5	5
	344	**394**	**440**
Current Liabilities			
Trade Creditors	552	645	733
Other Creditors	119	137	157
Accruals	39	39	39
Taxation	151	219	267
Wages Control Account	72	80	90
Loans& Hire Purchase	83	83	83
	1,016	**1,203**	**1,368**
Working Capital Ex Cash	**(671)**	**(809)**	**(928)**
Bank Current Account	313	857	1,528
Long-term Loan	**26**	**26**	**26**
Net Assets	**(97)**	**232**	**671**
Share Capital	59	59	59
Reserves	(156)	173	612
	(97)	**232**	**671**

Cash

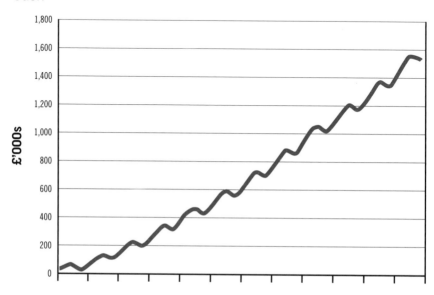

Your turnover will be £3 million to 15 million, largely depending on the sector you are in, and profits will be between £200,000 and £1 million. Crucially, you will be able to calculate the numbers as being the product of key drivers, supported by results to date.

Key drivers are those that shape the other performance numbers. In the illustrations on pp.187–88, the number of units is a key driver – the more units we sell, the more members we have. The number of units per manager or supervisor is also a key driver. The more units per person, the more profitable we are, until we reach the limit of a manager's capacity.

Once you have arrived at this point, your business is scalable. This means that if you repeat what you have been doing, you will continue to generate sales and profits. If you, or the new owners of the business, invest to create greater capacity so that these actions can be repeated by more people over a wider area, the business will generate proportionally more sales and profit.

> ▸ Imagine an online retailer that sells fashion clothing over the internet. It can build its business by spending on marketing to attract new buyers. The process is clearly defined and the number of customers can be forecast with some certainty, as past experience makes the relationship between marketing activity and sales consistent and predictable.
>
> ▸ A professional services business finds new clients through recommendations from existing clients and by marketing. The number of new client relationships that comes from each area of activity – and their average value and duration – can be predicted, based on past experience, though the value of each unit sale is likely to vary far more than it does for the online retailer.

I mentioned earlier that profits can go down as well as up, in the early stages of a business, and I'm aware that I haven't demonstrated this. If that's what you think will happen, it's absolutely fine. In the old days, when manufacturing was common in the UK, businesses invested in assets and their plans showed increases in profits. But in today's IT and service-based business world, most of the costs of expanding are likely to be expenditure, shown as

> Profits can go down as well as up

costs in the P&L, rather than as investments in fixed assets that appear in the balance sheet. These days, a plan that shows break-even or losses for one or two years, followed by real growth as the returns from marketing, development and other expenditure start to kick in, is perfectly acceptable, and won't deter discriminating investors. Even lenders, who are more cautious, will fund the working capital requirements.

Once you can see with reasonable certainty that you will achieve profits in six to 18 months' time (for example, because you have won a contract this autumn that starts next April), you will be able to sell the business. But long before you make that sale, while you are still working towards it, you should work out how much you are going to need.

Working out how much you need

Having got the business into a shape where it is growing and can be sold, we can take the next step towards making this a reality. To do this, we will need to find a price that's acceptable to the buyer and to you and the other sellers.

The price that will work best for you, I suggest, is *not* the biggest amount you could possibly get if everything kept on growing.

It's the amount you need for it to feel like enough.

It's the amount – and you can calculate it quite objectively – that will give you financial independence, satisfy your needs and provide those things you really want, rather than all those millions of things that you would quite like to have.

This amount can be calculated as follows:

1. A house.

plus

2. An additional sum for things that will happen for a while, but not go on year after year, such as school and university fees, and for the one-off luxuries you really want, like round-the-world trips.

plus

3. A capital sum to live off.

adjusted for

4. The amount you wish to pass on.

less

5. What you already have.

less

6. What you may inherit.

> The price that will work best for you is not the biggest amount you could possibly get if everything kept on growing

Let's look at each of these, and the **caveat** – what happens if you get divorced.

A house

Houses (or flats) represent many things to us – security (including privacy and safety), homeliness (warmth and comfort), status (maybe a statement of who we are), investment, and location (usually proximity to work and schools, sometimes to relatives). I suggest that, in order to achieve WealthBeing, only security and homeliness really matter. When you have sold your business, the location of your home will no longer be governed by proximity to work. When school routines come to an end, where you live can be determined by where you will feel homely and secure.

Using these as your only criteria is important, because house values are largely driven by location – especially proximity to commercial centres and good schools. Even if you sell the business before the children have left school, your calculations should be based on the value of the house you will buy to live in after they've left.

The value of the house will be after paying off the mortgage. So if the value of the house you intend to buy is £800,000, this can be achieved by selling a house with a value of £1 million that has an outstanding mortgage of £200,000 (ignoring fees and stamp duty).

A house that fulfils these criteria is simply one that you enjoy living in, with enough rooms for you to pursue your activities, in a place that fits your lifestyle. There is scope here for a bit of dreaming – of swimming pools and stables, or of second homes so that you can be handy for the West End theatres *and* go for country walks. No-one is saying you shouldn't have these things, but I am taking this opportunity to ask you to consider them fairly carefully:

> A house… is simply one that you enjoy living in with enough rooms to pursue your activities in a place that fits your lifestyle

- ▸ Swimming pools are expensive and time-consuming to maintain (you don't hear people in the UK say they miss having a pool, but I know several who regret that they do have one).

- ▸ Second homes are much more expensive than even luxurious hotel holidays, and also tie you to one particular place.

- ▸ Larger houses are usually just that, larger, but with the same functions as the home you left behind.

It's well worth taking some time to think about what it is you actually want, rather than what you think you want or what you feel will look good. Examining your lifestyle now, and considering how it might be when the business is sold, is the best way of making choices that will suit you and your partner.

You may see your current house as an investment, and a tax-free one at that. I would still consider the house you want to live in and put down the money you are likely to need for that. If the house you currently own happens to be worth more than the house you want to live in, so much the better. Put down its value, in your calculations, as part of the amount you already have, and the difference will reduce what you need to get from selling the business.

An additional sum

Everyone wants to have treats, to feel special and to turn dreams into reality. At times, maybe when funding a new car or paying out for a holiday for a growing family, being able to treat yourself can seem like a very distant prospect. And it will recede even further into the future if you choose to fund some or all of the children's university costs. But further reflection may lead you to see things differently. There are other considerations you may not have thought of:

- University (and school) fees are finite.

- Luxuries can cease to be so desirable once you've experienced them a few times. I'd be surprised if you get as excited now about going out for dinner as you once did. And the same applies to bigger, grander experiences – familiarity does breed contempt, to some extent.

- There will always be some things you dream of having, when you have reached a milestone or can afford them. In my experience, we rarely get round to doing all of them. And, again, when we look carefully, we often find that our desire for them is not that strong.

Years ago, I promised myself I'd buy an Aston Martin if I successfully sold Gordon Durham & Co. When it was eventually done, I celebrated by going for (another) test drive. But, maybe because I could now appreciate that the sale itself had met my need for self-esteem, I realised that I no longer needed this obvious trophy as a reward. So I thought about the practical limitations of an Aston Martin – size, primarily, plus overpriced parts and ridiculously short intervals between services – and settled instead for an Audi. I'm still very happy with it.

I suggest you write down everything you can think of, and apply the 3Ds:

1. **Dream** a bit – look at each one and imagine what it would feel like.

2. **Discuss** it – hear how it sounds to you, and what your life partner thinks.

3. **Decide** – choose the treats that feel right for you.

> WealthBeing also means finding wealth's ceiling and so creating space to satisfy your higher needs

The capital to live off

When we're employed and we get a pay rise, it often seems, within a month or two, that we couldn't live without it. Material wealth satisfies our physiological needs (food, shelter and health), gives us safety and some independence and may improve our social connections, thus covering several of the lower levels of Maslow's Hierarchy of Needs. But achieving WealthBeing also means finding wealth's ceiling, and so creating space to satisfy your higher needs.

To calculate the amount you require to meet the wealth need of WealthBeing, you should estimate what you must have to live on each year, ignoring the luxuries you have just listed:

ITEM	£'000
Utilities/ Council Tax/ Insurance	7
Health Insurance	3
Two Cars (depreciation/fuel/repairs)	10
Food	10
Holidays	5
Hobbies (golf, sports club)	5
Clothes, Shoes, Going Out	20
	60

You will probably disagree with the figures I have chosen here, but this table gives you a format to help you capture what you spend, or think you could spend, every year. You don't have to analyse all your bills, though what you currently spend is easily derived from bank and credit card statements. What you could spend is, obviously, limitless, but I've arrived at this total of £60,000 based on responses from people I know who enjoy a comfortable level of family living in the London area.

It's also worth noting that we tend to spend less when we get older, though the cost of living will increase again when we need the services of a care home or nursing home. Private homes cost from £25,000 a year for care to about £50,000 a year for nursing and the average length of stay in both care and nursing homes is two to three years, though a quarter of these older people will stay longer and a few will keep going for 10 or 12 years.

You will also be entitled to a state pension, as long as you have worked for at least 30 years. There are big changes happening in the pension system, but the basic figure will be £7,700 a year when you reach the pension age (probably 67 for you, dear reader), from 2016 onward.

To receive £60,000 *after tax*, you will need an income of at least £70,000 and possibly as much as £83,000 *before tax*, depending on whether you are able to split the income between two of you and whether or not the amount you receive is subject to income tax (dividends) or capital gains tax (cash from the sale of shares or unit trusts).

The next step is to calculate the capital sum that will provide this. You need to know how much money you will need to produce this income of £70,000 to £83,000, allowing for inflation, until you die. This will depend on the real rate of return on your investments, which will be made up of two components:

1. The return is made up of the current income paid out, plus any growth in your investment's value, as a percentage of the starting value.

2. The real return is this return, adjusted for inflation.

Studies of investment performance over more than six decades, analysed by Thomson Reuters and Barclays Capital and collated by Saul Djanogly of the Investment Fitness Club, show that real returns after inflation have been between 3% and 7% p.a. on average, before costs. The key determinant of return is the mix between bonds and equities in the portfolio – the higher the percentage invested in equities, the higher the long-term return (but the higher the short-term losses, too, when markets turn down):

▸   A 100% investment in equities (stocks and shares) that's held for at least ten years has provided a 7% real rate of return, on average, with the worst ten-year periods showing a loss of 4% and the worst single year leaving investors with losses of 32%.

▸   A 100% investment in bonds has produced positive real rates of returns of 3%, on average, with the worst ten-year period showing a gain of 2% and the worst single year bringing losses of 5%.

In calculating the amount you need for WealthBeing, I am going to assume a mix of bonds and equities that, based on those statistics, should give you a real rate of return of 5% p.a. over ten years. As with any investment advice, these figures are not guaranteed (share prices may go down, as well as up, as the regulators insist on warning us). But again, as all investors do, we shall rely on them, in the absence of anything better!

Before putting these figures into the WealthBeing calculator, we need to deduct the cost of managing your portfolio. This is discussed more fully in the following chapter, Deepening and Caring for Your WealthBeing. For the time being, though, we will take it as 1%, leaving us with a real rate of return, net of costs, of 4%.

What you pass on

You will have all this capital, increased by inflation over the years, at the end of your life. To find the amount you need to realise from sale of the business, you need to decide whether you want to pass all of it on to your beneficiaries or if you are prepared to use some of it up yourself. It's natural to begin with the assumption that you should give as much as you can to your children, to give them the best possible start in life. But, as with many principles we have looked at in this book, this thinking may require refinement.

Think about this. Few people are made happy by being given a large amount of money. You are not the only one who wants to achieve something significant with your life. So do your children, to a greater or lesser extent. My children have asked me not to pay off their student loans, even though press comment on the issue always seems to assume that those who can do this will. Handing over a substantial amount of cash, at

> Few people are made happy by being given a large amount of money

an early stage, can make the recipients feel their own efforts in life are being diminished. If the amount you hand over is really large, the feeling can be quite belittling.

Clearly 'large' is a subjective matter. But I'd suggest that anything more than £1 million is large, by any standards, and anything over £100,000 for someone under 40 is probably in the same bracket.

On the other hand I am not a fan of handing over nothing – the 'I did it the hard way and so should you' approach.

My observation of people who adopt that attitude is that the struggle has hardened them and made it more difficult for them to connect with others. That, of course, is the very antithesis of what WealthBeing tries to achieve. Gifts or soft loans of £10,000 to £100,000 are what you needed when you were starting to get going, and they are the best way of helping those around you.

The amounts I'm talking about in this book are not on the same scale as those made by Scottish billionaire Sir Tom Hunter or by Warren Buffett. But Sir Tom quoted Mr Buffett and I will, too: 'Leave your children an amount so that they can do something, but not so much that they will do nothing.'

Whatever you decide to do about your will, I suggest you talk about it with your beneficiaries. Death may not be the scariest thing, but it is still a big taboo – and discussion of wills seems to fall into the same category. But this logic is faulty. People I've talked to who deal with bequests, in the antiques and fine art business and in charities, tell me the situation always seems to be happier when the beneficiaries and family are not surprised by the contents of a will. If you aren't inclined to think about your will and discuss it well in advance, you might want to ask yourself why that is? What's stopping you from setting out your plans in this area as you have in other areas of your life?

What you already have

Your existing assets will usually consist of three elements:

- ▸ Equity in your house.

- ▸ Savings, including pensions from previous employments, buy-to-let properties, and assets or investments owned by your partner.

- ▸ Surplus assets in the business.

The first two of these figures should be easy enough to pin down, though valuing the pension needs to be handled with care:

▸ Should you or your partner be lucky enough to have a defined benefit pension, it will take time to get the figure and you will be told an income figure, rather than a capital sum. What you want to know is the income with inflation included, and the best figure to adopt is the amount available at age 55, which will be the most conservative figure. Deduct this from the income figure that you feed into the calculation, then add to the capital required one year's income for each of the years between the sale of the business and your 55th birthday.

▸ If you are in a defined contribution scheme, use the current value of your fund (any figure from the last 12 months will be good enough).

Now let's think about the surplus assets in your business. Growing the company will require cash, as we have seen, and taking money out will always reduce the business's growth possibilities, by reducing its ability to deal with short-term crises and restricting the amount others will be willing to lend. So there is a tendency to keep the money in the company to cover emergencies, in the early days, and then, later, to leave it there because of the tax charge that will arise if you take it out. When the business is sold, it is acceptable to take out what is not required. To work out how much this could be, you need to calculate a couple of key figures:

1. The amount of working capital there is in the business, and the amount of borrowing available to finance it.

2. The amount of cash left after.

    a. Using up this working capital finance.

    b. Paying off cyclical creditors. Cyclical creditors are those that are not always due and are paid off at regular intervals, such as Corporation Tax (annually) and VAT (every quarter).

What you may inherit

Realistically, you could also deduct money you expect to receive as an inheritance from your parents or grandparents. But people are reluctant to discuss these things, and you may not know how much their estates will be worth or even whether you are a beneficiary. Just asking the question may cause offence. If you'd still like to include a figure in your planning, here's a rough and ready calculation you could use:

▸ Estimate the value of the house, and assume that they will spend all the other assets.

▸ Assume the first £650,000 will be tax free, since this is the threshold for a couple for inheritance tax.

▸ Deduct 40% from any amount above this.

▸ Assume the resulting figure is shared equally among the children. If you are doing this in relation to grandparents, repeat the process of subdivision until your share reaches you.

Results

There is a calculator on the WealthBeing website (www.wealthbeing. co.uk) that allows you to specify the amount you need, the investment yield expected, the amount of capital you want to pass on and the time period over which you will use up the remainder. This time should be the rest of your life, from the date that you sell the business. There are many quick calculators on the internet to help you to do this – my favourite is the interactive lifespan tool from Northwestern Mutual, which shows you a running calculation of your life expectancy, changing all the time as you answer basic questions about your health, habits and family background. The classic method is as follows:

▸ Subtract your age at the time of the sale from 100. So if you're 41 now and it will take seven years to create, nurture, develop, expand and sell the business, you'll be 48 at sale. Take this away from 100 and you have 52.

- Divide this figure (52) by 2, which gives 26.

- Add this figure to your age at sale, which gives 74.

It is now possible to work out how much you need to sell the company for, by adding up the elements we have discussed here and dividing by two fixed percentages:

1. The percentage of the company that you own.

2. The rate of Capital Gains Tax. If you sell shares in a private company, provided you have 5% of the voting rights, the rate is 10% for gains of up to £10 million. This is the rate we'll assume.

The net result of all our calculations is illustrated in this example:

STEP 1	A HOUSE		£'000	
	Value of House Desired		800	
	Stamp Duty	1%	8	
			808	808

STEP 2	ADD ADDITIONAL ITEMS	£'000	
	School Fees	30	
	University Fees	50	
	Weddings	25	
	Other Celebrations	20	
	Once-in-a-lifetime Experiences	50	
	Treasured Possessions	100	
		275	275

STEP 3	HOW MUCH WILL YOU SPEND EACH YEAR?	£'000
	Property Running Costs (utilities, rates, insurance, repairs)	7
	Health Insurance	3
	Travel Costs (depreciation, fuel, servicing)	10
	Food	10
	Holidays	5
	Hobbies/gym	5
	Drink, Clothes, Entertainment	20
		60

STEP 4   HOW MUCH INCOME IS THAT BEFORE TAX?

Band £'000	No. of Earners No.	Total Band £'000	Tax Rate £'000	Post-tax £'000	Pre-tax £'000
10	2	20	0%	20	20
32	2	51	20%	40	50
Excess	2		40%		

Note: National Insurance is ignored since income will be unearned   **60**   **70**

STEP 5   HOW MUCH CAPITAL IS THAT?   £'000

		£'000	
Income Required		70	
Real Returns on a Mix of Equities & Bonds	5.0%		
LESS: Management Charges	-1.0%		
Real return after charges	4.0%		
Capital required to produce income of £	70,000		
Of which part in perpetuity	50%	875	
Number of years for balance (life expectancy)	26	559	
		1,434	1,434
TOTAL REQUIRED			**2,517**

STEP 6   DEDUCT CURRENT SAVINGS/FINANCIAL ASSETS   £'000

	£'000	
House Value	800	
Mortgage	-400	
Pension Fund	100	
Other Items	50	
Surplus Cash in the Business	100	
	650	-650

STEP 7   DEDUCT EXPECTED INHERITANCES   £'000

	£'000	
Her Relatives	200	
His Relatives	200	
	400	-400

STEP 8   CALCULATE VALUE REQUIRED FROM BUSINESS

SUM OF STEPS 1–7 GIVES NET VALUE REQUIRED FROM BUSINESS	1,467

STEP 9   VALUE OF BUSINESS REQUIRED   £'000

		£'000
% shareholding	65%	
Capital value of company after Capital Gains Tax		2,258
Capital Gains tax (applying Entrepreneur's Relief on gains up to £10 million) at	10%	
SALE VALUE REQUIRED OF COMPANY (before Capital Gains Tax)		**2,508**

REQUIRED PROFIT OF COMPANY		£'000	
	Sale value of company required	2,508	
	Multiple of maintainable earnings	5	
	Maintainable earnings required		502
ADD:	Reasonable remuneration of managing director	75	
	Profit before taxation and owner's remuneration required	577	

It's also worth noting what you will have available to pass on to your beneficiaries, either at death or before that time. The example we have used produces the following result:

BALANCE REMAINING AT DEATH OF SURVIVING SPOUSE (IN CURRENT-YEAR VALUES)	
	£'000
Capital Not Used Up	875
House	800
Treasured Possessions	100
Inheritance Tax at 40% on amount above £650,000	-450
	1,325

I understand that making predictions about the rest of your life is not just a numerical exercise. What happens if you live longer, spend more, get seriously ill, need to be in a nursing home or find yourself in some completely unpredictable set of circumstances? There are three things to consider:

1. You have a reserve – the 'Balance remaining at death of surviving spouse' – which you can dip into if necessary. You can also release some of the money tied up in your house, under certain circumstances.

2. Don't just rely on one calculation. Leave it for a few weeks and do the figures again. Do the sums several times. Write down the result each time and you will notice that the variations between the answers will gradually become less. A pattern will emerge as you say to yourself 'That won't happen.' You will reach your own boundaries.

3. Err on the upside and research the things that worry you, such as nursing-home fees or the cost of adapting your house if you become handicapped. The differences to the outcome will be fairly small. For example, nursing-home fees for market leaders are up to £50,000 a year. So if, as in our example, expenditure per person is £30,000 (half of £60,000), you'll need an extra £20,000 of capital for each year you or your partner are in a home. According to BUPA, only one resident in 40 stays ten years or longer. So the additional requirement to achieve this would be £200,000 each, or £400,000 for both of you (which is very unlikely). That's just 22% of the capital remaining at death shown in the example (which is £1,775,000 *before* Inheritance Tax). It's also worth stressing that we tend to spend less as we get older and the amount of expenditure you have put down is probably an over-estimate for your later years.

4. While tax rates may change and tax incentives may provide opportunities to improve the numbers, I have ignored these. If rates change significantly, it's because everything else has changed. Systems have a habit of balancing themselves, so the net return will probably be roughly the same, and new tax incentives will not make a big difference to the overall picture. When discussing plans with a qualified financial adviser, keep sight of the big picture (which we'll look at in the next chapter) and don't chase opportunities that seem attractive because of the tax advantages. The key to sanity and peace of mind is to make sure your investments are as sound as your business.

Caveat

If there's one factor that could affect these figures significantly, it's divorce. Ideally, you won't get divorced, because many of the principles I have set out apply in your primary relationship, just as much as they do in business. I am grateful to Andrew G Marshall, probably the leading British marital therapist and author on the subject, for his sensitive and enlightening work on this topic. He says that problems can often be managed better, so that divorce is avoided, if both people involved acknowledge and act on the following ground rules and assumptions:

1. I'm not your boss (nor vice versa), but we can still agree, assent or amend. Assent here means that we disagree, and that's OK.

2. I am on my journey and you are on yours. We are in a joint endeavour, but we are separate. A degree of separateness, and looking after yourself, is not only a fact but an essential element of a healthy, loving relationship.

3. Our emotional reactions are 80% the result of associations with past events, largely experienced in childhood, and only 20% about the current issues. So I accept your feelings as valid, but they are not my feelings. I didn't have the same past experiences as you, and so I can react differently to the issue at hand.

4. Whatever the issue is, it's 50% down to me and 50% down to you. None of us is perfect.

5. We should start to deal with our issues by asking questions, not by trying to act straight away to resolve them. Let's explore the alternatives before acting on them.

If discussions with a marriage guidance counsellor fail to lead to acknowledgement and action, you may feel the relationship is at an end and that it's appropriate to seek a divorce. I am divorced, and I vividly remember meeting a solicitor for the first time to get the legal advice I needed.

'There are no rules in divorce,' she told me. 'Whatever you think will apply may not!'

Emotions run high and making rational judgements is naturally hard for both parties, despite the best efforts of lawyers and mediators. But applying the principles we have discussed, especially thinking win-win and focusing on the facts, should help you to find your way to a settlement. The process is likely to involve working through several steps and holding fast to the most important priorities:

- ▶ The children come first. It's now becoming generally accepted that divorce doesn't necessarily harm children, but bad divorces (and bad marriages) in which the children are fought over do. So make sure that arguments do not involve them. The courts will see their needs as paramount and make sure that they have a home, food, clothing and all the things they are accustomed to, as well as access to their parents as they wish.

- ▶ If the marriage has been short, things should be relatively simple. You should usually be able to take back the assets and liabilities you brought in and share 50:50 any joint assets (which will be small), subject to providing a house and funds to care for the children. In this case you can keep the business, or your share, anyway: I know several instances of couples that are in business together and are now divorced.

- ▶ In longer marriages, lasting several years, you will share the assets and liabilities 50:50. While there are some economies in day-to-day expenditure that arise from sharing a house with someone, these are quite small in proportion to the sums we're discussing, so having half the assets to meet half the expenditure still holds true. The exception is that you'll need somewhere else to live. In situations where one partner owns the business, the business owner will usually keep the shares, while the other partner keeps the house. So you may need to add the cost of another house to the figure you have arrived at. Alternatively you can add another spouse or life partner. I have remarried and my new wife acquired our house as part of her own divorce settlement.

- ▶ There is also a requirement to maintain each other in the manner to which you have become accustomed. You can take into account existing salaries or, where one spouse has been out of the workplace, potential salaries. You can also apply the savings that have been built up, including pensions, to help to meet this.

Unless you had a pre-nuptial agreement listing what each party brought into the marriage and what each will take out, it's possible to argue over everything. Both spouses can find themselves claiming that this or that asset existed before the marriage, or came in via inheritance, or was the result of exceptional efforts by one party or the other. But there are exceptions to these exceptions, which judges, mediators and arbitrators use to achieve fairness (which is the stated legal principle). For someone engaged in seeking WealthBeing, the eventual settlement is likely to look something like this:

▸ The business goes to the spouse engaged in it.

▸ The house goes to the primary carer of the children.

▸ There is an agreement that both spouses will work to look after themselves.

▸ There is a transfer of a balancing sum, or agreement to ongoing maintenance payments, to ensure that each person can live without major changes to his or her lifestyle.

The 'answer' will be the original WealthBeing sum (reduced because of the fact that you are not at that point yet and so the expenditure requirements will be current reality, not that which is hoped for), plus another house or spouse!

The biggest issue is often the time and energy required to get to this settlement. The stress of fighting your ex-lover reduces your effectiveness considerably. During the two years in which our negotiations went on (and this was through mediation, not the full adversarial court process), I was effectively unable to grow the business. It was all I could do to maintain it, though this was in 2008 and 2009, so the recession was probably another factor.

The less emotion there is involved in divorce negotiations, the easier it is to achieve the legal aim of fairness (which is an unemotional concept), and the more likely you are to get a settlement both parties can accept without lingering regrets and resentments. Once again, and here it may be harder than in any other area of your life, win-win is your aim. The more support for this you can glean from other aspects of the WealthBeing journey, the easier it will be to apply.

How to get it

Now that you can clearly see how much you need, you can work towards getting that cash sum.

The most straightforward way to do this is to continue to earn more than you need and save the balance. This will take quite a while, but is doable in a stable business sector. It's how some people working in finance, the media and the professions expect to get wealthy. Their earnings often exceed £100,000 and they invest the excess. They make the most of this by using tax reliefs for pensions (£40,000 p.a. tax free at the moment), ISAs (£11,000 p.a.) and maybe using the EIS (Enterprise Investment Scheme) or its younger cousin, the SEIS (Seed Enterprise Investment Scheme), for some high-risk, high-return investments, which will give them 35%+ tax relief on their investments and allows gains to be taken tax free, subject to complying with fairly detailed sets of rules.

But unless your net income is much higher than your expenditure, this takes a long time. A requirement of £1.5 million, as shown in our example, would take 30 years of saving at £50,000 a year. And to save £50,000, you would need an income that was £83,000 more than expenditure. If you're aiming for expenditure of £60,000, you would need income of £153,000 (£70,000 to give you £60,000 after tax, plus £83,000 for the savings). Architects, accountants, lawyers, doctors and vets can all plan this realistically, but it's a lot of years and, as I said, all business sectors change over time. For example, the legal profession is suddenly facing the challenge of open competition in many of its services (including bread-and-butter earners like conveyancing) as well as the fact that information that law firms used to charge for is now freely accessible online.

So the plan must still be either to sell the business or, possibly, float it on the stock market. I advise against flotation for two main reasons:

1. The business needs to be worth at least £50 million before it is really a viable option. While entrants are often smaller than that, their experiences during and after flotation are usually chequered. A business smaller than that doesn't have the spread of investors or financial and management resources to deal with short-term market fluctuations.

2. More importantly, the founder and senior management find it hard to realise their investments. In fact, directors often find themselves locked in by rules and practices that discourage or prevent the sale of significant stakes. You could find that the only way you could achieve WealthBeing was by being taken over, which is, after all, a type of sale.

So the last remaining option is to sell the business. The process I recommend involves just four steps:

1. Appoint an agent.

2. Find buyers.

3. Negotiate a price.

4. Sign a contract.

I've heard it said that only 35% of potential business sales arrive at a successful completion. When this process is followed, the chances of success increase greatly. Let's look at each component.

Appoint an agent

I used to work in corporate finance, so I understand the ins and outs of selling a company. Despite that, there are two reasons why no business owner, even one who understands the process, should ever contemplate selling a business without an agent:

1. I don't know how to look for purchasers. Neither do you. I don't maintain databases showing company profiles that might pinpoint potential acquirers. Nor do you. You may be aware of some competitors and bigger companies for which your business might be a logical addition, but you don't know all of them. As I have said, when talking about your business being an asset, rather than an income stream, some acquirers will have needs you are unable to even imagine. An experienced business agent understands this and will be able to maximise the number of interested parties, even if these potential buyers don't actually recognise how your company could fit their needs.

The first interested party I was introduced to when selling Gordon Durham & Co was a property maintenance business. Though we were doing a lot of refurbishment work, the two activities were not the same. The potential purchaser was changing lightbulbs and tidying gardens, while we were tackling larger, higher-value tasks, such as fitting kitchens and putting in new windows.

I couldn't see the relevance, but the agent correctly guessed that the potential buyer might be interested in moving up the value chain. Nothing came of the approach, but it taught me to respect the agent's ingenuity and professionalism.

2. More importantly, I could not approach potential acquirers, even if I could find them. Ringing strange companies and offering to sell them your business sounds odd. And it is! It's better all round to use an agent. The agent is also useful throughout the process, as a means of moving things along without giving the impression that there is any desperation involved. Undue haste can be unnerving to a buyer, but coming

from an agent it is seen simply as a desire to get paid, as the bulk of the agent's fees depend on a successful deal being done. Fees are not low, for this reason. A ballpark figure would be £5,000 to £25,000 up front plus 5% on the first £1 million of sale value, 4% on the next £1 million, tapering down to 1% for everything above £4 million.

The agent will write a selling document (usually known as an Information Memorandum), which describes your business as it is and outlines its potential. Agents will ask lots of questions (if they're any good) and by the time they've finished with you, you will probably feel rather paranoid. Many parts of the conversation are likely to end with a non-committal 'I see' from the agent, when you have just explained another low-margin contract or a potentially awkward compromise agreement. But remember, no business is perfect. It may be pointed out to you that the net profit of the business is equal to the profit from only one customer or even just one contract.

> Remember, no business is perfect

Equivalent but not equal. It's an argument I have heard from time to time and it may make you feel that the business is not so valuable, because profits look to be based on one deal. But it's not true nor is this 'equation' uncommon so acknowledge the comment but don't act on it.

Alongside the IM, there should be another document that relates the amount of capital required to the company's growing profits. This is done as follows:

- ▸ Divide the capital value required by the earnings multiple. Profits are income and the value of the business is capital. The earnings multiple converts one into the other, and it's the last key component in agreeing a sale. We will look at it in detail in the section on negotiating the price.

- ▸ There will be another important figure, often referred to as 'future maintainable earnings'. This is the profit for the current year before tax and before paying out anything to you and the other shareholders, but after paying someone a salary to take over the management roles you perform. It's likely that this salary will be less than you pay yourself, because part of what you give yourself is due to your ownership of the business.

▶ Compare the future maintainable earnings figure to the profit before tax and before your remuneration shown in your results and forecasts. It needs to correspond to the profits shown for last year, this year or next year.

The result, using the example profits and amount required set out earlier in this chapter, looks like this:

	£'000
SALE VALUE REQUIRED OF COMPANY	2,508
Multiple of maintainable earnings	5
Maintainable earnings required	502
Add: Reasonable remuneration of managing director	75
Profit before taxation & owner's remuneration required	577

COMPARE PROFITS REQUIRED WITH THOSE ACHIEVED & FORECAST	Last yr	This yr	Next year
	£'000	£'000	£'000
Profit Before Tax	240	453	599
Add: Owner's Remuneration	78	85	90
Profit before taxation & owner's remuneration achieved/ forecast	318	538	689
Profit before taxation & owner's remuneration required	577	577	577
Is profit achieved/forecast greater or lesser than profit required?	Lesser	Lesser	Greater

I have assumed here that only you are a director and only you are exiting the business, and that your partner is staying. If your partner is also a director and leaving, his or her remuneration needs to be included at each stage (under 'reasonable remuneration of a [sales] director' and 'owner's remuneration').

The financial results, in greater detail, may look like this:

PROFIT & LOSS ACCOUNTS

Activity	Item	£'000	Comments
	Sales	4,700.0	
	Cost of Sales	-2,846.0	
Gross profit		**1,854.0**	
Staff	Admin, Service, Marketing & Sales People	-900.0	People costs are roughly 2/3 of overheads
Marketing	Travel & Subsistence	-100.0	
	Adverts, Events etc.	-50.0	
	Website	-40.0	
Premises	Office	-75.0	
IT/Comms	IT	-45.0	
	Phones & Internet	-35.0	
Admin	Insurance	-35.0	
	Financial Control	-60.0	
	Audit & Consultancy	-20.0	
	Sundries	-41.0	
Profit/(Loss) Before Tax & Directors' Remuneration		**453.0**	
	Director's Remuneration	-85.0	
	Tax	-73.6	
Retained in the business		**294.4**	

BALANCE SHEETS

Item	£'000	Comments
Fixed Assets	.0	
Debtors	850.0	
Creditors	-528.6	
Working Capital	321.4	In most businesses this will be about 5% of sales now
Cash at Bank	70.8	**You'll need a facility based on detailed monthly forecasts to cover short-term fluctuations**
Loan From You	.0	
Net Assets	392.2	
Share Capital	30.6	
P&L Account	361.6	
Net Worth	392.2	

If you can achieve a result like this one, where this year's profits are very close to what you need them to be and next year's are forecast to be higher, you can proceed to market the business with a realistic chance of getting the sale completed.

Find buyers

If you're going to sell the business, you need to find someone who wants it. Often acquisitions are described to purchasers' directors or shareholders as 'platform', 'gateway' or 'strategic entry' opportunities, or as offering products that are 'complementary to your existing range'. In other words, there is the promise of something they can refashion or integrate in order to achieve their goals. These may include:

1. Adding your products to their range.

2. Stopping your products competing with theirs (they can close you down, if they wish, after they have bought you).

3. Gaining access to your intellectual property (sometimes a patent, but more often know-how or business relationships).

4. Scaling up to increase the profitability of their business by reducing overheads as a percentage of sales and removing duplicated activities.

5. Entering a new market that you are in, but they are not.

6. Getting your key people into their company (maybe the development team or sales force).

It is also helpful to show that you are one of the three market leaders. That's not as hard as it sounds. You just have to define your market carefully and tightly. Gordon Durham & Co was one of the three largest independent building contractors in the Northeast. Morgan may not be the world's mightiest car company, but it can certainly claim to be Britain's leading producer of handmade, open-topped, three-wheeler, twin-engined sports cars.

The financial press sometimes talks about other reasons for an acquisition, such as getting hold of a strong balance sheet or realising undervalued assets. Reasons like this tend to apply to large, diversified groups, rather than focused, growing businesses.

The agent will find potential buyers with needs like those listed and will act as the matchmaker, arranging an initial meeting. Yes, of course, this is just like a first date, with both parties unsure of what to expect, though what they have seen attracts them. The number of matches is correspondingly low, because they are probably not looking for exactly what you have to offer. They may be only

> Show you are one of the three market leaders. That's not as hard as it sounds

vaguely interested, at first, in what you can provide. Skilled agents will make sure that the matching criteria are clear, but no-one can account for how many matches they want, and which are most important – that indefinable element of taste and feel – and if you aren't what they are looking for, that will be the end of the relationship.

Such meetings are always going to be stressful. You may have seen bright, articulate people in the 'Dragon's Den' being completely tongue-tied in similar situations – Little Me meeting Big Them. If you can deal with that in your own way, that's great. If not, try either or both of the following:

- ▸ Breathe deeply. We have talked about meditation and relaxation before, and this is a time when it can be really useful. If you've been practising it, you won't need to disappear for 20 minutes to get yourself into the right place. Just pop out for a breath of fresh air, breathe and compose yourself and you will be able to perform well.

- ▸ Remember Mike Harding! You may not have heard of this comedian and folk singer of the 1980s, but his name will give you a hook to remember the other way of de-stressing yourself. Mike, a plain-speaking Northerner, used to say, 'If you're ever overawed by someone, just imagine them in the netty [WC] with their trolleys [trousers] round their ankles!' What he was saying is that they may have more money, status and power than you – or be its representative – but they are still human, with the same limitations and bodily functions. There's no need to treat them as different beings.

If these meetings go to plan (there may be several, as more people get involved or those higher up the chain get interested), it will eventually be time to negotiate the price.

It's obvious that the buyers will want to pay the minimum and you want to get the maximum. What is less clear is how you reconcile those positions and do the deal.

Negotiate a price

The price, as I've said, will be your profits times an agreed earnings multiple. But what profits and what multiple? There's a bit of a trade-off here. If you're using profits that have already been achieved, the multiple will be higher. If you're using profits that are forecast, the multiple will be a bit lower.

In nearly every case, though, the multiple will be between three and eight times these profits, because this equates to the price of a public company in your sector. Let me explain:

▸ Public companies' shares are usually traded at between eight and 20 times their post-tax profits, depending on their fortunes and those of the market in which they operate. The first thing to look at is which market you operate in and what multiples apply to companies in your sector. You may be able to see more than one sector that applies to you. Scanning the financial pages, or talking to colleagues, you may also be aware of companies with multiples of 20, 30, even 50 times profits. These outliers do exist, but they are the product of exceptional circumstances, such as a worldbeating product (Google) or a new CEO moving in from, say, BP, with global ambitions for a small company – as happened when Tony Hayward joined Genel Energy. Where this kind of calibre is involved, these multiples are attainable – but they are rare.

▸ Still, public companies are less risky to invest in than small private ones – they are much bigger and the shares can be bought today and sold tomorrow. It is generally accepted that the ratings of private companies should therefore be 50% to 60% lower than those of comparable public companies.

▸ Since the earnings multiples, known as price/earnings (P/E) ratios, for public companies are a multiple of their post-tax earnings, we need to convert them into pre-tax multiples. To do this, we reduce them by 20%, the rate of Corporation Tax.

Reducing typical public company P/E ratios by 50% and then by a further 20% gives a range of 2.5 to 8. As with most statistics, the outer limits are less common than the middle of the range. Timing is very important, as these ratios alter significantly as economic conditions change. The FTSE 350 (made up of the 350 largest companies quoted on the London

> Leave something for the purchaser

Stock Exchange) was priced at around 16 times post-tax profits in early 2015. Back in July 2009, just after the crash, it was priced at around ten times post-tax profits.

Armed with the IM, a profit record that you have reasonable confidence in, and an understanding of earnings multiples, you can move towards negotiating a price. Serious negotiators will start by offering you a reasonable figure of, say, four times last year's profits. If they buy and sell companies, they'll know all this stuff, and since you are working with an agent they will expect you to be properly briefed. If they want the deal to go ahead, they won't antagonise you by starting with a silly offer.

But this offer is unlikely to be acceptable – and a deal won't be agreed until you have had a face-to-face meeting. Clearly this is very important to you, and the purchaser knows it. My suggestions for dealing with the negotiations are based on my own personal experience:

▸ Leave something for the purchaser. They may be a public company with a market value of more than 12 times earnings (post-tax profits), but that doesn't mean they will pay 12 times your earnings (or 9.6 times maintainable pre-tax earnings) for your business. They need something to justify the purchase in the beginning, something that will increase earnings, and something to allow them to invest to get the business fitting snugly into their group or company. So leave something, but not a lot.

▶ Be clear about the lowest price you will accept. Consider carefully what's a sensible multiple for your sector and how achievable the growth you've forecast really is. Does it rely on the business getting a lucky break, or is it just repeating what you have been doing for a while? The work you have done to date will support this greatly.

▶ Don't go it alone. Have someone else in the room on your side – the agent or an accountant or business partner – so that you have time to think.

▶ You are being watched closely, so try to stay relaxed. Don't twitch at key moments.

▶ Know when no means no. One useful trick is to deliberately call the negotiator by the wrong name, at the first meeting. Watch the reaction, and learn it. That reaction is what that individual will give out when he or she means no.

▶ Don't get to no too quickly. These deals have several components and there is usually room to trade, giving away what is less important to you but significant to them, and vice versa.

▶ Take time-outs if you need to. They're not a sign of weakness. Quite the opposite, in fact.

In the end, you must be prepared to leave, if you are not going to get what you are looking for. Unlike trading relationships, these deals are one-offs and a win-win is harder to shape. You want the maximum cash, and reasonable assurances about the future of the employees. They want the lowest possible price, and freedom to manage the business. Brinkmanship is common, and saying no is just part of the game. Leaving is more significant, but may still be just part of the game. Leave in the best possible way, so as to keep the door open for further negotiations.

When I sold Gordon Durham & Co, I realised a deal wouldn't get signed until I said no, and was seen to mean it. I had spent three hours going round and round the terms, while the other side tried to reduce the price. I even heard, or thought I heard, one of the negotiators say 'The Income Taxes Act doesn't apply to Corporation Tax' (it does), at which point I judged that logic had left the building and they were just pushing me to see what my limit was.

I looked at the 6ft 6in CEO and said, calmly, 'We have £5 million in the bank and £2 million of property and our forecast has gone up 50% since we started negotiating. You want another £50,000 reduction. That is not acceptable, so there is nothing more to say, except that I wish you well.'

As I left, I thought I could see the fear in his eyes (because he would have to report to his boss that he had lost the deal). We concluded the sale just two days later, when the other side agreed to my price, subject to some of the money being retained for a period, in case we breached our warranties (which I'll come on to later).

I'd like to round off this section with a note about selling software businesses. Though software people like to talk about multiples of turnover, this is just a shorthand way of calculating a price in a business where the cost of making the product is tiny and even sales and admin functions can be largely eliminated, so that sales turnover and profits are almost the same thing. If the software is a unique and fully protected item that can work worldwide for a global corporation, and your company has only been trading for a few years, turnover may be what's needed as the basis for calculating the price. But there will still be a calculation somewhere that shows the return to the purchaser on his investment net of all costs.

A successful negotiation will produce an outline agreement, usually called Heads of Terms. It sets out the price and other main conditions, including salaries for key employees and any specific items that have been agreed, such as the way surplus cash will be calculated when the deal goes through. This is not binding, but it is helpful, a big step on the way to concluding the sale, and enables you to progress towards signing a contract.

Sign a contract

There are two parts to this, which often occur in parallel:

1. Due diligence.

2. Signing all the paperwork, of which the Sale and Purchase Contract (SPA) is often only a small part.

Due diligence, or DD, as it's known, is the process by which you assure the purchaser that all is as it seems. The purchasers will take a detailed look at the accounts and other matters that they consider important, such as customer contracts, patents and trademarks and systems design and documentation, as well as employee records, bank loan agreements and property leases. The list can be long and scary, so you need experienced professional advisers who know how to handle this. Accountants often act for purchasers, so they are the best people to employ when you are selling, because they know what the purchaser is doing and what is expected.

No-one expects the business to be perfect. There will be items, especially when it comes to tax, that haven't been considered fully, since they are only relevant when it comes to selling the business. Capable advisers will help you navigate through all these, maintaining the confidence of the purchaser all the while. Few problems are insurmountable, though there are four particular elements that will always ring alarm bells if they are revealed for the first time during the due diligence process:

▸ Being sued, on a significant scale.

- ▸ Losing bank funding.

- ▸ Tax issues that are ongoing or have resulted in fines.

- ▸ The loss of a major customer.

Even these can probably be overcome in due course. It's the fact that they are unclear at the time at which you are passing the risks over to someone else that may hold the deal up or stop it being done.

When selling Gordon Durham Holdings (the holding company of Gordon Durham & Co), we had an issue with the tax treatment of the shares I had issued to our senior managers. The company's tax adviser said there was no solution, and that they would have to pay income tax at 40% on their share of the proceeds, rather than Capital Gains Tax at 10%.

Rather than accept this, and the end of the deal, I contacted the specialists at BDO who had set up the share scheme. They reorganised the shares and got clearance from HMRC and the sale was able to go ahead.

If there is a major problem, consider how to resolve it before presenting it. Your customers may be worried by the prospect of a change in control of the business. Sometimes their contracts will even include the right of termination if there is a change of control. Check their contracts, and meet them face-to-face, so they can see you are genuine when you reassure them that the deal will not be harmful to them.

In my experience, all deals are 'off' at least once.

Miscommunication produces an apparent impasse, with grim assertions that there is no way one of the parties is going to move. The party in question may not even be the buyer or the seller. We could be talking about key employees, customers or suppliers – often a bank – who can all get involved and say no.

What they usually mean, though, is 'Tell me more' or 'Yes, at a price', rather than no. So deal with it. The longest negotiation I was involved in took 12 months, because there were no face-to-face meetings and communication became steadily worse and more confused. If your talks are becoming protracted and the problems aren't being resolved, insist on face-to-face meetings or change your advisers. The worst scenario of all occurs when the purchasers are being badly advised. When that happens, they won't agree what is reasonable and you can't tell them how unreasonable they are being, because they are suspicious of your motives: 'Well, you would say that, wouldn't you?'

You may be wondering why I haven't mentioned lawyers yet. This is because, if they are brought in too early, they hinder, rather than help, the process. There are two reasons you need to be aware of:

1. While there is currently a move towards fixed fees, lawyers generally much prefer to be remunerated for time spent, rather than results achieved. So there is a mismatch, from the outset, between your objectives and theirs.

I once heard people from one legal firm earnestly discussing how to deal with 'the paper clips'. In the end, it was a slightly comic incident, as what I'd overheard turned out to have been a conversation about pay-per-click results.

2. The lawyers nearly always see their role as negotiating hard to get the best possible deal terms, including the best price, for you. And who wouldn't want that? Er... you. The overriding aim must be to get a deal done – an agreement that's acceptable to both sides. Asking for something that is not acceptable to the other side will only antagonise people and could be fatal to the whole negotiation.

I once asked for advice over the wording of a Heads of Terms agreement and got it back redrafted because the lawyer was supposedly 'improving the deal for you', even though the changes he was inserting would clearly have been seen as unacceptable.

Obviously, this is not always the case, but it is something to be aware of, and it's not confined to inexperienced people. Both your lawyer and the other side's lawyer will (or certainly should) have negotiated the sale and purchase of businesses before, representing both purchasers and sellers, so both sides should have a feeling for what will be acceptable to both parties and what won't. You should also be aware that some purchasers will send in a solicitor to present outrageous demands while everyone else hangs back and waits to see if you will bite, all the while professing ignorance of what is going on.

If you get the right advisers on both sides acting on properly prepared letters of engagement, you should be able to agree a contract, the Sale and Purchase Agreement, which captures the terms set out in the Heads of Terms and sets out warranties and indemnities – promises by you and all the shareholders that what you've said about the business is true. In addition, you will have to sign a disclosure letter where you disclose any exceptions to the absolute statements in the contract. For example, there may be a warranty that there have been no claims for unfair dismissal. Your disclosure letter may have to state, for example, that the office manager claimed sex discrimination when she wasn't able to return to work two days a week and that the dispute was finally settled on payment of £10,000.

It is possible to get insurance against a claim being made, but such policies usually depend on you being totally and unreservedly honest in the first place and claims are very rare. If you yourself have been misled about the state of a property or a particular customer relationship – either deliberately or inadvertently – it's hard to see what you can do. In practice, therefore, I have serious doubts about the value of these policies.

A word may be appropriate here about the position of your other, usually minority, shareholders. If the company has been properly set up, there will be provisions in its Articles of Association which stipulate that minority shareholders cannot block a sale, as long as they receive the same price per share as everyone else. If not, you will have to use persuasion (or change the Articles to include these provisions, known as 'drag along and tag along'). The minority shareholders will normally be asked to give the same guarantees about the company as you and could also be asked to guarantee 100% of the loss if things go wrong (the technical term is 'joint and several liability'). It is hardly ever appropriate for them to give a 100% guarantee and only appropriate for them to give percentage guarantees at all if they have been directly involved in the management of the company or are married to a person who has.

It is impossible not to be distracted by the sale process. But as long as you are able to keep at least one eye on the business and stay calm and focused on what you want, you should eventually get to the situation where all the warranties are properly supported, the disclosures have been clearly made and accepted, and an appropriate set of board minutes has been drafted. With luck, this can all be done in about three months from the date of the Heads of Terms document. At last, you will have a contract in front of you that you can sign.

It is impossible not to be distracted by the sale process

WealthBeing check

Here's that familiar WealthBeing graph one more time, updated to reflect this final stage of progress towards your ultimate goal:

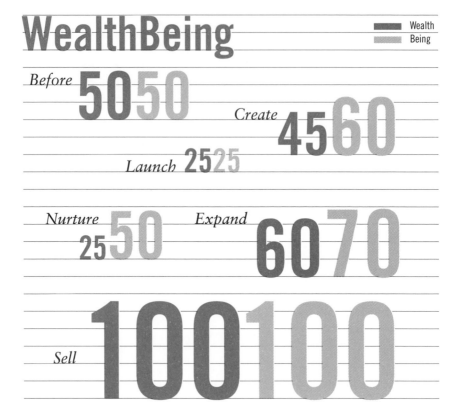

We set out your wealth requirement earlier in this section, so you should be able to tick that off, even if the final result is slightly below your projected result. As we noted in making the calculations, this is an art, not a science. The important thing is that you have now realised your wealth, turning it from potential into hard cash.

The feeling of achievement at this point is about as good as it gets. My own experience when selling the family business was one of deep satisfaction, of having achieved my destiny, which was to use all my skills to hand it on to a company far better able to run it than I and my relatives could, in return for the best price possible.

The journey had taken me 19 years, not five, and there had been many setbacks along the way. But the desire to make a difference meant that I stuck at it, and I won. Not every battle, of course, but the war – the series of challenges, issues and problems that had produced a result in my favour. And in everyone else's too: win-win-win.

This wasn't just about self-esteem, having overcome all the obstacles through a combination of technical and emotional skills, but a real feeling of 'cognition', as Maslow called it, of doing something meaningful and having done the right thing for everyone. I had scaled the heights, become free of superficial material worries – and taken a big step towards self-actualisation, free of all significant concerns.

We are all fundamentally insecure, but, when you get here, the fact that you have achieved this means that you will be more highly regarded by others. There may be some who grumble – those who didn't want you to sell the business, or maybe partners who thought that now was not the right time or that you could have got more. But the fact remains that you have achieved *your* goals of sufficient wealth and that priceless feeling of wellbeing.

So what now? Most business guides stop here and wave you goodbye to go your own way. But, in some respects, your journey is only just beginning.

In some respects, your journey is only just beginning

7

DEEPENING AND CARING FOR YOUR WEALTHBEING

Introduction

It may be that the deal requires you to leave the business at sale, but this is not always so. In fact, I would say that it only applies in about one case in three.

▸ You will probably be needed for at least three months, to make sure no-one gets spooked and runs away (not just employees, but customers and suppliers, too).

▸ If the deal is an earn-out, with payments made after the contract is signed that are calculated by reference to the profits earned in future periods, you may be there for several years. If the earn-out doesn't work out – there is too much interference or external conditions change – you can choose whether to fight or just walk away. Generally, the instinct is to hang in there and fight for what is yours by right. But you are in the powerful, privileged position of having a choice. You can choose whether to engage in expensive litigation, where the outcome is always uncertain, or simply decide to accept what is on offer, since it is already close to what you need, and get on with the rest of your life.

Eventually, you will get to the end of a journey you embarked on all those years ago. How many years is hard to say, which is why I haven't included any prescriptive timings in each section. The bare minimum is three years, but FD Solutions has been going for over 20 years, and Gordon Durham & Co was well into its seventies before it was sold. Whatever the time scale, at some stage your involvement in the business stops and a void opens up in your life, sometimes quite suddenly.

This chapter sets out ways of dealing with the big question of what your life can be now and how to decide what to do next.

Finally, it deals with how you can stay wealthy by looking after the wealth that's now yours.

Wellbeing: your life after selling the business

So what will you do now? Freedom to choose what to do is a privilege that's given to only the select few. I suggest there are three major steps to making the right choices for you:

1. **Wind down,** before you even think about winding up again.

2. Examine your needs, compare them with **your activities/intended activities** and see if they are genuinely aligned.

3. Think about your continuing purpose in life. When we have the freedom to choose, nearly all of us find that part of what we want to do is to serve others.

Winding down

The immediate aftermath of the sale will usually be full of celebrations with your ex-colleagues, special trips with your loved ones and the pleasures of acquiring the treasured items you included in the WealthBeing calculator. But after every high there must be a low, and it needs to be carefully managed.

The stress that's built up during the process of achieving the sale will undoubtedly manifest itself in a need for rest. Take a holiday and learn to really relax. It often strikes me as odd that Western cultures always see relaxation as an activity. The need to be busy is virtually an endemic disease. Other cultures put less emphasis on it and suggest that being and living in the moment is better. I hope that by now you have seen the benefits of meditation, of learning to concentrate on what is happening here and now. When we looked at it before, it was in order to help keep the pressures you were feeling under control, and to enable you to see and manage conversations. Now you have a chance to enlarge your scope and develop your ability to simply be. Take a look around and fully appreciate everything that's around you. If you think you already do, try this. It may make you think again.

Get a single raisin – yes, the dried fruit – and take a good look at it. Look at it closely for a minute, a full 60 seconds. Hold it close to your ear and rub it between your fingers, while you listen to it. Then smell it, and when you are able to describe its aroma with all the complexities of a fine wine, put it in your mouth (but don't chew). Feel it on your tongue, roll it around and appreciate its unique texture. Finally, when you can feel each little wrinkle and indentation, bite into it and taste the juice coming from it, making you salivate slightly. Chew the raisin as slowly as possible, then gently swallow.

This five-minute sensory exploration exercise will go some way towards reminding you how much we usually miss in the pell-mell of our daily lives. Paying fierce attention to the detail of your immediate experience will help you recalibrate your senses and enable you to gain a deeper appreciation of what you have achieved.

While you are fully in the moment and not embarking on another journey, it's an ideal time to have a thorough health check, too. Comprehensive health checks are a good idea, but are not generally available on the NHS, so we tend not to have them in the UK. But the arguments in favour are pretty compelling. The cost is low (about £400 for a two-hour 'mid-life MOT' consisting of more than 30 tests and assessments) and the health check will give you information about yourself that can be used, in consultation with your doctor, to guide you in any lifestyle changes you may need or wish to make.

There is a real risk that the need to wind down may overwhelm you. I've seen it happen to some extremely energetic and dynamic people, when they took their feet off the gas. You no longer see any real

> There is a real risk that the need to wind down may overwhelm you

need to get up – and when you're up, you find watching TV the most exciting thing you can manage. If this is the case, you may be suffering from depression.

Depression affects 30% of the population at one time or another, so it's by no means rare, and it is an illness, not a personal defect. Its causes are many and varied and you may have already encountered it, as I have. The biggest battle with depression, in my experience, is admitting that you have a problem. Once you have admitted it and seen a doctor, the cure can be administered. There are many drugs to combat depression, and some of them have been used and refined for so long that their side effects are limited and can be dealt with successfully. If you're still reluctant to address the possibility, look at the website Time to Change (www.time-to-change.org.uk), which aims to provide tools and other support for those who find it difficult to believe that depression may be affecting them.

When you're in a clear frame of mind, it's time to examine your needs and actions.

Match your needs and activities

You have earned the freedom to choose what to do next, so spend it wisely. But how do you decide what is right for you? I suggest three methodologies, two of which we have already looked at:

1. Revisit Maslow and his Hierarchy of Needs.

2. Revisit the idea of flow.

3. Find your mojo.

I hope by now you're familiar with Maslow's thesis. I suggest that WealthBeing is likely to meet much of your need for esteem and a good deal of your need for cognition (the meaning of life) – it certainly did for me. I also suggest that its impact on the remaining three high-level needs (aesthetic needs, self-actualisation and transcendence) will influence what you do next. If it has made you feel that you have found beauty, truth and goodness and that you have realised all your potential and would like to guide others, I suggest that you will be best served by doing it all over again – either starting another business or getting involved with those that do, as a business angel or similar.

In the Expanding It chapter, we looked at flow, the way of feeling union with your environment and enriching oneself. I asked you to move on from the activities this represented and become a leader, in order to create the wealth you seek. If you were engaged in activities that gave you this feeling, and you miss it, then you can re-engage in them.

But if you feel that building a business has only partly satisfied your higher Maslow needs, and if you didn't find any activity that truly made you feel in flow, then I suggest using a tool created by Marshall Goldsmith for his bestselling book *Mojo: How to Get It, How to Keep It, How to Get It Back When You Lose It.* Set out a two-by-two chart with happiness and meaning on the x and y axes, as shown below, and plot the activities that you have done and those that you would like to try. They can be as big or as small as you like. Those in the top right-hand box (meaning and happiness) constitute success (in your terms). Those in the bottom right (happiness, but not so much meaning) stimulate you. Those that appear towards the top left (meaning, but less happiness) are sacrifices that you choose to make. Those without meaning or happiness are the things you do just to survive. Activities where meaning and happiness are roughly equal, those in the middle, are especially sustaining.

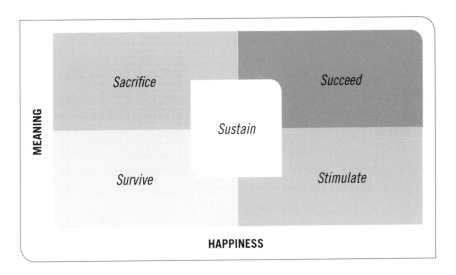

At this point, you might be asking: 'If building a business and selling it doesn't allow me to meet my higher needs or find my mojo, and it even stops me being in flow, then why should I do it?' My answer is that while it may not provide a complete sense of wellbeing, it provides a complete sense of wealth, enough wealth for you to be able to pursue other activities that meet your needs, as well as improving your wellbeing. The feeling of safety and security that this brings allows you to pursue your higher needs, which will often involve a desire to help and serve others.

You would probably recognise, too, that it was, at the very least, a stepping stone. You took a step from your old life, which was not fully satisfying, to one that produced greater satisfaction and enabled you to move on further.

Serving others

Rousseau said that we are all part of a social contract, that 'Man is born free, but everywhere in chains', and that is everyone's experience most, if not all, of the time. We have obligations, and we deal with others on the basis that if I do X, you will do Y in return. When this doesn't happen, disputes arise.

Even when the results are good – we trade, build and sell a business and accumulate wealth and wellbeing – they are still bounded by this limitation of mutual obligation. So moving outside that must be a new experience and can be desirable.

Furthermore, I have observed that when people relax deeply and visualise what they might do with their lives, they almost always say that they will give freely, in some way.

Now that your economic needs are met, you have the opportunity to give advice and assistance when you are completely unaffected by the outcome. Working for a cause, such as Amnesty, where you gain no direct personal benefit (since you have not been tortured or imprisoned), or supporting your child in choosing any career or life partner without any comment, are examples of how to serve others. Doing these things, without any vested interest in the outcome, can produce feelings of real joy. At the time of writing, I am the treasurer of a small charity, the Madrinha Trust, which mentors students in the developing world. Writing to our students and receiving their words back, in which they share their hopes and fears, gives us all a feeling of joy that comes from simply being ourselves and offering our experience and wisdom purely for their benefit. Unconditional, unselfish giving like this helps to make the world a better place. The fact that we feel good, too, doesn't diminish this.

Staying wealthy

It won't surprise you to know that, once you have received a large sum of money, a lot of people will suddenly want to get to know you better and be keen to offer you an even better life than you already have. I think I received seven invitations from NetJets for a private jet charter, alongside the many offers of concierge services, platinum credit cards and so on. Some of these may be on your once-in-a-lifetime list. But if not, be careful – they may make you feel you haven't got enough. I suggest going back to the WealthBeing calculator, looking at the luxuries you listed there and fulfilling those, or maybe replacing one with another.

Then turn your attention to managing your wealth. If you have decided to start another business, you should put some or all of the capital aside to do this. If you have decided to pursue other interests, you will need to invest your money so as to get the returns we assumed when working out the amount you needed to get for the business. To do this, you will need to look at four things:

1. Advisers.

2. Asset types.

Be careful – sales people may make you feel you haven't got enough

3. Structures and fees.

4. Risk, returns and timing.

Advisers

As with selling the business, I recommend working with an expert, in this case an independent financial adviser (IFA), rather than doing it yourself. These professionals should pay for themselves by maximising your returns and minimising the costs, especially tax. Your IFA can ensure that you get the maximum relief from each of the tax incentives that are available – pensions, ISAs and Enterprise Investment Schemes are the main ones. The other thing an IFA should manage is how the investments are held. I said that you shouldn't let the tax tail wag the investment dog, but your IFA should be able to tell you whether your investments will attract capital gains tax at 28% or income tax at 20% or 40% and make sure that the holdings are suitable for your tax profile.

Building the business required you to form relationships with people who held similar values to you and shared your win-win ethos. Selecting an adviser is no different. As technology has become cheaper, there is a growing number of small companies that have similar values to yours, and that have succeeded by following most, if not all, of the principles set out in this book. This like-mindedness means that you are more likely to feel comfortable dealing with them. As long as you take the precaution of only dealing with a regulated Chartered Financial Planner, you should be able to feel confident of receiving honest, professional treatment and sound advice, if you follow these two pointers:

- ▸ These IFAs will not usually have direct access to your funds, which are held in nominee accounts with organisations such as Old Mutual, except to change the holdings and to receive their fees. So the risk of your funds being diverted is as small as it can be, whereas using large 'one-stop shop' investment organisations doesn't offer the same protection. I know of one poor chap whose bank lost a million quid! They found it eventually.

- ▸ Discuss economic and political trends with your adviser, to find out if the IFA can see the bigger picture, and act accordingly. For example:

> Find out if the IFA can see the bigger picture

○ People in the more prosperous developing countries now want things which they can afford for the first time, including designer clothes, fine wines and foreign holidays.

○ Healthcare for ageing populations, genetic engineering to cure diseases and new technologies like 3D printing are also areas where demand can only increase. Investments in well-managed businesses in all these areas should produce good returns, as the markets develop.

Asset types

There are eight main types of asset, which I shall list in order of liquidity (with the assets that take longest to buy and sell shown first):

1. Shares in private businesses.

2. Specialist asset classes, such as art, wine, stamp collections and vintage cars.

3. Property.

4. Structured financial products, which are a mixture of stocks and shares, commodities and derivatives.

5. Commodities, such as gold (which can now be traded virtually, via the new ETCs – Exchange Traded Commodities).

6. Quoted shares and bonds (government bonds – gilts – and corporate bonds, which are loans to companies).

7. Derivatives.

8. Cash.

In order to invest in different asset classes and still have a sense of wellbeing, you need to understand how they work, and be advised by someone who can explain them to your satisfaction. Let's see how this works in practice:

- If you're investing in private companies, the risks can be high. I suggest that you only ever invest in a sector you have worked in and that you understand fully. I was once the finance director of a company in the software services sector, and I have made good returns in that area. When I've dabbled in other sectors, it's been disappointing every time. And it's not just me. The scariest example is the sausage manufacturer I mentioned before who put all the proceeds from the sale of his business into a restaurant – and lost the lot in six months.

- Only invest in specialist asset classes if you have studied them as markets. A love of wine or an appreciation of Cubist painting is not enough of a qualification. It is often the opposite in fact – a banker who loves Delft china bought a friend's antique shop, and it hasn't made a penny since.

- If you're investing in property, you need to understand the location you're putting your money into. In London, for example, some successful developers stick to one postcode, or even a few particular streets.

> If you're investing in private companies, only ever invest in a sector you have worked in

- The other classes are financial and the only ones that are sufficiently comprehensible to a new investor, and on which you can get satisfactory advice, are quoted shares and bonds. I have bought structured products (once, and once only) and looked at derivatives and had made up my mind – even before the financial crash – that they were not things I wanted to put my money into. The aim of derivatives (options and other devices) is to move risk around – I think these shares will go down and you think they will go up, so let's each reduce our risk by creating options for me to sell them to you. They don't create wealth overall, as if someone wins, someone else must lose. So I could never feel assured that investing in them, even as part of a portfolio, would produce a positive return. Prices of stocks and shares, on the other hand, are based on the performance and prospects of companies and their markets. This is what we have been looking at, and it's something we are familiar with. There's a lot of discussion in the media about every aspect of shares and markets, so it is possible for you, as a non-specialist, to be well informed and get good advice about something you understand. The next question is how you will go about it – the structures, returns and fees.

▶ Only keep in cash what you need to live off for a year or two and for anything else you have planned for that period. Cash doesn't produce the returns you can get from stocks and shares, but it is what you need to pay the bills. By keeping this amount as cash, you can choose when you sell shares and do it when prices are good, rather than being a forced seller because you need the money.

Structures and fees

There are three structures that allow you to invest in stocks and shares:

1. You can invest directly and build your own portfolio of shares, or use an adviser who recommends which shares to buy (and can do the buying and selling for you).

2. You can invest indirectly – buying portfolios of shares in open-ended investment companies (OEICs, or 'oiks', commonly known as unit trusts) or investment trusts, which are run by fund managers.

3. You can invest in portfolios of shares that have been set up to match the performance of an index, such as the FTSE 100, and are not actively managed. These are called tracker funds.

The first two methods involve other people who are engaged to maximise returns. They charge management fees of around 1% for doing this and usually charge a small fee (up to 0.1%) for buying and selling shares for you. The tracker funds are set up to be 'dumb'. They don't try to beat the stock market's total returns, but to imitate it and track its performance by holding a basket of the shares that make up the FTSE or whichever index you choose to track. Their management fees are significantly lower, in the range of 0.2% to 0.5%.

Beware of funds that say they are actively managed but are not noticeably different from tracker funds, except in the additional fees that they charge. Saul Djanogly, of the Investment Fitness Club, and others have examined funds, by looking at how much their returns vary from the index, to see if they really are actively managed or just say they are. Unfortunately, there are quite a few funds that fall into this category. There is a useful tool to guide you in this area on my website (www.WealthBeing.co.uk).

> Only keep in cash what you need to live off for a year or two

Beware of managers who switch shares often ('churning'). It's not necessary and it generally doesn't produce good results for investors, if only because the transaction fees can knock 0.1% to 0.25% off the returns.

There are now a variety of tracker funds that will track a personalised 'index' that you make up yourself.

In addition to the fees charged for buying and selling shares, you will need to pay your IFA. These fees used to be hard to discern and were a percentage of funds invested. Often they were paid by the investment managers out of their commission, making them even harder to quantify. The UK's recent Retail Distribution Review has ended this opacity, so you can now see who is charging what. Your own adviser should be charging on a time basis and making sure that you comply with the various regulations. The IFA will charge something – usually about 2% of the funds you invest – for giving the initial advice and setting things up, plus an ongoing fee of about 1% per annum. The original investments will probably be made over a few weeks or months, to smooth out any short-term fluctuations.

Risk, returns and timing

In running a business, the way to reduce risk is to manage everything that is within your control. In investing, very little is under your control – you hand over some money and wait to see it grow. So how are you going to do this and maintain a sense of WealthBeing? I suggest a two-stage approach:

1. Find a risk/return position you are comfortable with.

2. Take a position that suits your situation with regard to timing.

> The one thing you should avoid is planning to ride out a crash and then having to get your money out

As we saw when working out how much you need, the more risk you are prepared to take, the greater your exposure will be to potential returns and to possible losses. There is no right answer, just the one you feel most comfortable with. Your IFA will use a fact-finding questionnaire to determine your attitude to risk and will then be able to create a portfolio that matches this, since shares, OEICs and tracker funds also have their own risk ratings.

Some people overlay this with complex versions of portfolio theory, looking at returns from different assets in different market conditions and matching them up so that if one goes down another will go up. For example, if share prices fall, the value of government gilts will invariably rise.

The end result is a mix of shares and possibly bonds that matches your risk profile, reflects the trends that you and your IFA have identified and has an appropriate cost structure.

The final aspect of investment concerns timing. In my experience, it's likely that returns will be less than you expected in the first year or two. This is because the initial costs associated with making the investments have to be recouped from growth in the shares.

As time progresses, your returns should move towards the level the you set as your target (4%, 5%, 6% or 7% after inflation and before charges) and may, with luck, exceed them. The next question to address is when, if ever, you should pull your money out of shares and switch into cash or bonds. What is your attitude to timing?

The common view among fund managers, financial commentators and IFAs is that you can't improve your returns by timing moves to cash or switches from one class to another. They have statistics on their side, and they say that while you may not be able to see the top of the market, you can't see the bottom either. So whenever you move out of the market, you probably won't move back in at the right time and won't match the returns of those who stay invested through the ups and downs.

That may be so, but it won't stop you feeling that you can beat the market, or looking to someone to manage the situation for you when you want them to – springing into action on your behalf when you pick up the phone and say, 'I think the euro is going down the pan and I want to be out of the market.' You may be wrong, but you're entitled to feel and act this way. If you do, I can suggest two ways of deciding when the timing is right, one at the macro level and one at the micro level:

1. At the macro level, I would recommend 'the rule of 20'. This states that a market is fully valued if the sum of its P/E ratio and its dividend yield exceed 20. We looked at P/E ratios when we were discussing negotiating a price; dividend yield is the dividend that a company pays out as a percentage of the share price. Both figures are readily accessible in, say, the *Financial Times*, under the FT All Shares Index. Just note that they don't grow together: if prices go up, the P/E ratio goes up, too, but the dividend yield goes down, because its denominator, the share price, has increased.

2. At the micro level, I suggest that you can pick up signs that the stock market is overvalued from spotting particular assets that you think are priced too high.

In June 2007, my colleagues at FD Solutions were asked to help a company float on AIM (the Alternative Investment Market, the junior market of the London Stock Exchange). This company had few assets, made no profit and was run by one man whose objective was to create a whole new product about which he knew very little. This 'bargain' was valued at £4 million – not a lot for a public company, but a valuation that bore no relation to its current position. On seeing this, I moved my whole pension fund out of the stock market and into cash.

In 1989, as finance director of a plc, I was asked to assess the possible acquisition of a hotel group. Its annual profits were 6% of the proposed price. At that time, interest rates were sky-high – above 10% – which meant we could earn a guaranteed 10% without the business risks of running any hotels. The valuation of the hotel group was based on the assumption that hotel rooms were worth £100,000 each (and produced returns of £6,000 p.a.), but it was clear to me that they weren't. In 1991, when another recession hit, the Official Receiver suddenly became the second-largest hotelier in Britain.

There have been economic cycles of boom and bust for as long as economics has been able to measure them. Nothing that I have seen or heard persuades me that the world has changed and that we now have a new economic model. Despite people's claims that it was impossible to see the crash coming, it was inevitable, because so many assets were clearly overvalued. And there will eventually be another one, sooner or later. You can ride it out or try to manage your way through it. The one thing you should avoid is planning to ride it out and then finding yourself in a situation where you have to get your money out during the worst of the downturn.

The final way of dealing with risk is to accept a low rate of return but have it guaranteed, by purchasing an annuity. This involves handing over your capital to someone – usually a life assurance company – who will keep the capital and pay you an income for the rest of your life, regardless of how long you live. At the time of writing, annuities guarantee a return of 2.9% after inflation. It's not as good as you were planning, and if you die relatively young, it looks expensive. The rationale is that it's safer. You may decide you want to guarantee a portion of the yearly income you need, say £25,000 (inflation protected), in this way.

WealthBeing check

Wealth

Your wealth is now in the form of assets, rather than profits. So you should look for an investment report that demonstrates the returns you are getting, compared with inflation and the general growth of the markets. You need to collect the following data:

▸ Cumulative net returns (if you want gross, you can get costs from your IFA).

▸ Index returns.

▸ Inflation.

Tabulate it and you can get charts that look like this:

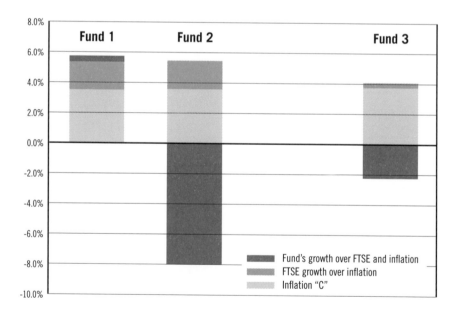

These charts show that Fund 1 is ahead of the FTSE (the chosen index) and inflation, that Fund 2's losses are nearly 14% compared with the index, and Fund 3 has grown, but not as fast as the FTSE, which itself has exceeded inflation.

The sample data I used is here:

INVESTMENT REPORT AT APR-14

FUNDS DATA		Fund 1		Fund 2		Fund 3
Date Invested		Dec-09		Jan-10		Mar-10
£'000 Invested		125		125		125
Additions		5		15		10
Withdrawals		(18)		(50)		5
Total £'000 Currently Invested		112		90		140
Current Value £'000		139		80		150
Months Held		52		51		49
Fund's Annual Growth 'A'		5.7%		-2.6%		1.8%

MARKETS DATA							
FTSE at Date of Investment	Dec-09	5,400	Jan-10	5,400	Mar-10	5,700
FTSE Now	Apr-14	6,627	Apr-14	6,627	Apr-14	6,627
FTSE Growth 'B'		5.3%		5.4%		4.0%
CPI at Date of Investment	Dec-09	111.0	Jan-10	111.0	Mar-10	111.0
CPI Now	Apr-14	127.7	Apr-14	127.7	Apr-14	127.7
Inflation 'C'		3.5%		3.6%		3.7%
Fund Growth Above FTSE & Inflation 'A–B'		0.4%		-8.1%		-2.3%
FTSE Growth Above Inflation 'B–C'		2.2%		-6.2%		-2.0%

Wellbeing

And your wellbeing will, I hope, feel like this:

A home ——————————————————

Capital to live off ——————————

Life's little luxuries ———————

Something to pass on ——————

————————————— *Safety*

————————————— *Esteem*

————————————— *Cognition*

————————————— *Self-Actualisation*

8

NEXT STEPS

WealthBeing is not the only way to live your life, but it is one way. This first edition of *WealthBeing* is my founding attempt to describe the situation where you have enough of everything you need, and then to guide you there. I am hoping its publication will draw others into sharing their experiences, so that we can form a deeper understanding of WealthBeing.

It's not easy, but it's not impossible. In essence WealthBeing is a combination of actions, thoughts and emotions that allows you to obtain the material rewards you seek in order to feel fulfilled while keeping you safe on the way there. Dreams are fun and visions are the next step, but it's only when you have turned them into reality that you can meet all of Maslow's Hierarchy of Needs.

I hope this guide will enable you to do this, that you can read it once or twice and then refer to it over the coming years to reassure yourself that you're still going in the right direction. Its aim is not to give you all the answers to every situation that you will encounter, which would obviously be impossible, but to guide you so that you know the direction of your journey and can spot the key signposts along the way. The website has many tools and resources to enable you to find the specific information and guidance you need to shape your own journey.

I hope you will now feel able to embark on that journey, supported from four directions:

1. From behind – you have something to refer to that gives you a good idea of what to do, and how you might feel if it goes wrong.

2. From below – the shared experiences of others who have tried, failed (ever failed) and succeeded have awakened your belief, so that you now think you can do it.

3. From in front – as you digest this information and start to consider your own path, the tools and tips will enable you to fill in a lot of the gaps until your future direction is clear enough for you to take that first step on the thousand-mile journey.

4. From above – in addition to the book and the website, there will be guides, people to watch over you and give you further guidance.

Of all the points we've touched on in this book, there are two I'd particularly like to emphasise:

1. Make sure that you do all the things we have covered, and do them, or make sure that someone else does them, well. If you concentrate on doing some of the things very well or perfectly, and fail to do other bits well, then success is unlikely. It's only when all the dots are joined up that the picture is clear.

2. Learn to recognise enough. Capitalism tempts us all the time with new things we might think we need to feel good. Until you recognise what is enough for you, and what feeling good is like, you won't have a sense of WealthBeing.

I wish you every success, combined with happiness, along your way.

9

GIVE ME THE GOOD STUFF

The key points of WealthBeing

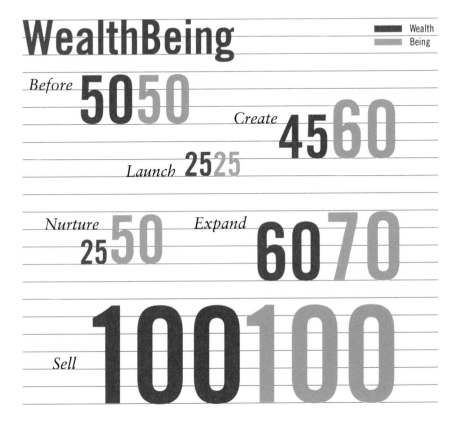

WealthBeing

■■■ Wealth
■■■ Being

Before **50**50

Create **45**60

Launch **25**25

Nurture 25**50**

Expand **60**70

Sell **100**100

Recognise yourself and your needs

WEALTH

You want a **reasonable amount of wealth** and the freedom that it brings.

You have or can acquire three attributes:

1. You know **how to win**

2. You want things to **be better**

3. You're prepared to play **the long game.**

WELLBEING

You want to fulfil all your emotional needs:

1. **Physiological**

2. **Safety**

3. **Love** and connections

4. **Esteem** (achievement)

5. **Cognition** (the meaning of life)

6. **Aesthetic needs** (beauty, truth and goodness)

7. **Self-actualisation** (realising your full potential)

8. **Transcendence** (guiding others).

Thoughts produce decisions.

Emotions produce actions.

Use these tools at **www.wealthbeing.co.uk**

WEALTH

Good information – only decide when it's clear.

Negative information – even the worst result is finite, not infinite.

WELLBEING

Good feeling – relax, and check what your body, mind, feelings and spirit are telling you.

Negative feelings – break the vicious circles by seeing why the problem is insoluble. Is it?

Maintain your morals – the world shares a commitment to seven values:

1. Honesty (integrity and truth)

2. Responsibility (promise-keeping)

3. Respect (equality, abiding by the law)

4. Fairness (impartiality)

5. Compassion (tolerance)

6. Love

7. Freedom.

Synchronicity – if you stay true to your path and open to the possibility of predictable miracles, they will occur.

Moderation – eat, drink, sleep and take exercise in moderation.

2 Create a product by bringing something new to what you know

WEALTH

Find a problem that is either:

1. A **severe** problem for a **few** ('I really need')

or

2. **Not too severe** for **many** ('We would like').

Either be **good at providing it**, or license it to a provider, or partner with the provider.

Make sure it can work **today.**

Make sure the **price** of the solution is **comparable** to other solutions and is **profitable.**

WELLBEING

Recognise that you are now **consciously incompetent**: you know what you don't know.

Recognise that **your dark side** will try to sabotage you. A **failure** to make significant progress will still be of **more value** to you than any costs that you've incurred.

Recognise that the idea is **your parents' delinquent grandchild** (bound to cause trouble) and **your life partner's stepchild**. They won't love it quite as much as you do.

Don't worry about the economy. Recognise that a **buoyant** economy is good for **sales** and a **depressed** economy is good for **costs.**

Be excited about **creating a business**, as well as solving a problem.

This is **your journey** and, if you are successful, the feeling will sustain you ever after. Even if you don't reach your intended destination, you will have learnt a lot that can be valuable to you.

Use these tools at **www.wealthbeing.co.uk**

WEALTH

Activity-based costing to understand prices.

Use savings or credit cards to fund the creation of prototypes.

A one-page business plan can capture:

1. **Sales, volumes** and **prices**

2. **Costs** and **capacity**

3. **Overheads** and other costs such as tax.

WELLBEING

WealthBeing will guide you in your learning.

Destroy a representation of your dark side.

Present your idea to **three** good friends (good **listeners with knowledge of the problem**) and ask them if they get it.

3 Launch it and feel a sense of achievement as you do

WEALTH

You will need up to **£50,000** for the business, plus income for your own expenditure.

If raising funds, the business is worth **£100,000 to £1 million.**

Find customers by **connections** through colleagues, contacts of colleagues or internet groups.

Demonstrate the **benefits** – show your product is either:

1. Faster
2. Better, or
3. Cheaper.

Get a specific buying signal or move on.

Build your database by getting details in return for information that is either:

1. **Technical** (how to)
2. **Tips**
3. **Teaser** (intriguing), or
4. **Take care** (warning signs).

People buy from those they like. Build **rapport**. Ask open questions.

People buy from those they trust. **Trust** = Credibility, Reliability and Intimacy, divided by Self-orientation.

Make **reasonable assurances**, but don't give cast-iron guarantees.

WELLBEING

Reducing personal expenditure gives the venture meaning.

Failure to connect with one prospect is an **event, not a trend.**

Price so as to **break habits**. Increase prices later.

Find a **partner or mentor**, so that, between you, you are good at inside, outside and the glue.

Work together for a **few months before** mutually committing.

If sales are few, either:

1. **Re-engineer** the product
2. Apply it to a **different problem**

or

3. **Congratulate yourself** for having the courage to try.

Try something different?

Treat yourself. This is the hardest part of the journey and you need a reward that doesn't undo the efforts you've made.

Use these tools at **www.wealthbeing.co.uk**

WEALTH

Sources of **funding.**

Calculate the **percentage** owned by **investors** as: investment required (grown by 30% p.a.) as a percentage of the value of the company in five years.

Corporate Cashflow Calculator

WELLBEING

Analyse what you **have to** do and what you **enjoy** doing.

Ways to build **rapport**:

1. Eyes **up** (visual) – 'I see'

2. Eyes **sideways** (aural) – 'I hear you'

3. Eyes **down** (touchy-feely) – 'I understand'.

Find **co-founders online.**

Find **mentors online.**

'Ever tried. Ever failed. No matter. Try again. Fail again. Fail better.'

4

Nurture it by making sure that it's GOOD

Then it feels good, too

WEALTH

Listen to what customers think. Make sure that it's **good**, but not necessarily perfect.

Tell stories about the **benefits** that you have provided.

In selling and networking, **listen**. 'In order to be understood, seek first to understand'.

Distributors are COWs: they have

1. **Capability**

2. **Opportunity**

3. **Willingness.**

You need to pull as well as push through channels.

Time is the **scarcest** resource **at this stage.**

Processes should be comprehensive: **what if... ?**

The culture of your business should **allow people to fail** occasionally.

WELLBEING

We are not judged by our **mistakes**, but by how we **deal with them**. Fix things so that it's good.

If you **push** me, I'll **push back.**

When negotiating:

1. **Think win-win.** It's the only way to maintain your morals

2. **Expect the unexpected**, but don't capitulate.

Look after your **diet, exercise and sleep**. Your energy is vital.

In the UK, people are **slow to change** their habits.

Critical thinkers recognise problems and help to resolve them.

When people start to **seek you out**, you get a surge of energy.

Get rid of **energy sappers.**

Use these tools at **www.wealthbeing.co.uk**

WEALTH

Communicate clearly with the 3As. Either:

1. Agree

or

2. Accept

or

3. Amend.

WELLBEING

Find support by mapping critical and committed:

1. Uncritical uncommitted – **Actors**

2. Uncritical committed – **Evangelists**

3. Critical uncommitted – **Sceptics/cynics**

4. Critical and committed – **Critical thinkers.**

5

Expand it by investing and leading

'The less I do, the more I get done.'

WEALTH

Invest to advance. Time is now more scarce than money.

Hire for attitude. Enhance existing skills, don't require different ones.

Build a team with **complementary skills.**

Lead/manage with **open questions.**

Manage by reference to a realistic **vision** and values that acknowledge all moral **values.**

Understand **who** uses the products and **how**. Grow sales by being **visible** and having conversations (rather than shouting).

Direct sell unless distribution will contribute more profit.

Keep control: choose suppliers who have similar values and always have direct, immediate control over production.

Keep overhead **costs variable.**

Understand the balance sheet and make sure you know how much cash you'll need, when, and in what form (asset based, loans or equity).

WELLBEING

Recognise the feeling of flow when you're busy in the business. Either feel it when leading the business or appoint a leader and create the role that suits you.

Confront the brutal facts, but never lose faith. Don't look to blame; acknowledge your own mistakes.

Have fierce conversations and if people don't change, ask them to leave.

Expect staff turnover as the nature of the organisation transforms.

Avoid fighting over contractual issues.

Look beyond the immediate situation to resolve problems (look through the fingers).

Go away for a day or two. Get some space and distance to make the problem seem more manageable.

Play the percentages. You can **choose** whether or not to be upset by a failure.

Talk to other CEOs, leaders, coaches and mentors.

Ask ten questions to change everything.

Use these tools at **www.wealthbeing.co.uk**

WEALTH

Myers-Briggs personality tests:

1. Get energy from yourself (**I**ntrovert) or others (**E**xtrovert).

2. Take in information literally (**S**ensing) or i**N**tuitively.

3. Make decisions analy**T**ically or by **F**eeling.

4. Deal with the outside world, decisively (**J**udging) or keep options open (**P**erceiving).

Create and track **values.**

After-the-event insurance.

Profit and cashflow forecast.

WELLBEING

Recognise flow. It's when you:

1. Concentrate on an activity that requires skill, has a clear set of goals and is bounded by rules.
2. Have sufficient skills, but don't find it too easy.
3. Need to concentrate fully, so that you lose track of time.
4. Get clear feedback on progress.

Use fierce conversations:

- My **issue** is…
- It's **significant** to me because…
- My **ideal** outcome is…
- The **background** is…
- **I have** done this, and thought that…
- The **help** that I'd like from you is… .

Ask ten questions to change everything:

1. In relation to your problem or issue, what are the three main barriers to progress?
2. Of these three, what is the one that, if changed, would change everything?
3. Just for now, imagine that you could change anything. In what ways would this one thing have to change to move your problem closer to resolution?
4. When you imagine that you have made these changes, how does it feel?
5. What, specifically, stops this from happening?
6. What would you have to do, or stop doing, in order to overcome this hurdle?
7. What stops you?
8. If you knew what to do differently, could you do it?
9. If you knew you could do it, would you?
10. When?

Supper Club, ABLE, Academy for Chief Executives, Vistage

Build it and sell it

'More entrepreneurs regret not selling than regret the price.'

WEALTH

Recognise the **business's limitations** – no business lasts for ever.

Identify your business's **unique place in the world.**

Ensure your **managers are independent.**

A strategic plan demonstrates a scalable business with realistic **results related to what drives** them.

Increase prices to reflect the greater strength of demand.

Provide new things in existing markets or existing things in new markets, but **not new things in new markets.**

Expand when it **adds value to your shares**, not just profit.

You need **a house plus £1–2 million** and a sum for one-offs, less what you already have or expect to inherit.

Appoint a **selling agent.**

Sell for **4 to 6 times** adjusted profit before tax (easier when stock markets are rising).

Sign **Heads of Terms**, *then* appoint **lawyers** to agree a contract.

WELLBEING

Recognise **your own limitations** – no-one lasts for ever and there is a **balance** between wealth and wellbeing.

Recognise that you are emotionally attached to the business, then start to **let go.**

Discuss who wants to stay and **who wants to go**, when the business is sold.

Work out **how much is enough**. Leave something for the buyer.

When negotiating the sale, **don't feel overawed.**

Be **prepared to walk out** of negotiations, but do it calmly.

All deals are 'off' at least once. Get experienced advisers and **communicate in person with everyone**, including customers and lenders.

If you divorce, you need either **another house or another spouse.**

Use these tools at **www.wealthbeing.co.uk**

WEALTH

Investment questionnaire:

1. If we spent £x in this way, what would the **additional profit** be?

2. Could £x be funded by the **profits** we are **already generating**?

3. If not, could it be funded by **borrowing** against unpledged assets we have or will have (such as debtors from future sales)?

4. If not, or if not entirely, we would need an equity investor to fund the rest

5. Compare the value of your equity before investment and after investment and borrowings.

WealthBeing calculator

Board agenda

WELLBEING

Mike Harding ('trousers round the ankles').

'I love you, but I'm not in love with you':

▶ **I'm not your boss and you are not my boss.** We can still Agree, Assent or Amend.

▶ I am on my journey and you are on yours.

▶ Our emotional reactions are **80%** the result of association with **past** events and **20%** related to the **current** issue.

▶ Whatever the issue, it's **50%** down to **me** and **50%** down to **you.**

▶ To resolve issues, start by **exploring** them, **rather than fixing** them.

Life expectancy calculator

Deepen and care for your WealthBeing

'Freedom to serve others is a privilege of few.'

WEALTH

Appoint an adviser who sees the **trends** in which you can invest.

Stick to **stocks and bonds**, unless you have experience of the other investment types.

Returns should be 2–5% after fees and inflation.

Look for signs of overpricing either around you or in the **rule of 20** (P/E ratio + dividend yield of a market should not exceed 20).

Manage your wealth and see its **returns clearly.**

WELLBEING

You'll need a **rest.**

Chew a raisin!

You'll feel low, eventually, for a bit. If this persists, seek help.

Acknowledge your achievement.

Appreciate the **freedom to choose.**

Appreciate the buzz you can get from **purely helping others.**

You can't **manage the highs and lows** of markets, but you may **feel better** if you think you have the ability to buy and sell when you wish.

Use these tools at **www.wealthbeing.co.uk**

WEALTH

Wealth report

Closet tracker questionnaire

WELLBEING

Time to Change, if you need help acknowledging and dealing with depression.

Use **Maslow's Hierarchy of Needs, flow** or find your **mojo**.

Map activities for **meaning and happiness:**

▶ Both = Success

▶ Meaning, less happiness = sacrifice

▶ Happiness, not so much meaning = stimulation

▶ Neither = survival.

And remember, business is always easy until you put numbers to it. Here are the illustrations of each phase, on one graph. The most important thing to note is how cash goes down in the first three stages, even when profits go up.

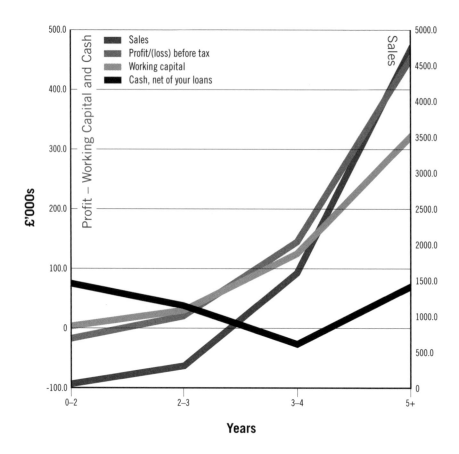

BIBLIOGRAPHY

CHAPTER

1   Stephen R Covey. *The 7 Habits of Highly Effective People*. 1989. Simon & Schuster, New York

1   Susan Scott. *Fierce Conversations: Achieving Success in Work and in Life, One Conversation at a Time*. 2003. Piatkus, London

1   Matthew Syed. *Bounce*. 2011. Fourth Estate, London

1   Abraham H Maslow. 'A Theory of Human Motivation'. 1943. *Psychological Review*, USA.

1   Rushworth M Kidder. *Moral Courage*. 2005. HarperCollins, New York

2   *Vital Growth: The importance of high-growth businesses to the recovery*. 2011. NESTA, London

3   Duke Corporate Education. *Coaching and Feedback for Performance*. 2006. Dearborn Trade Publishing, USA

3   Samuel Beckett. *Worstward Ho*. 1983. Grove Press, London

4   Dr Sharon Turnbull. *Harnessing Social Dynamics and Building Your Leadership Talent Through Times of Cultural Change*. 2008. Association of MBAs: Business Leadership Review V:II

5   Mihaly Csíkszentmihályi. *Flow, The Classic Work on How to Achieve Happiness*. 2002. Rider, London

5   Richard Barrett. *Liberating the Corporate Soul: Building a Visionary Organization*. 1998. Routledge, London

5   Jim Collins. *Good to Great*. 2001. Collins Business, New York

6   Andrew G Marshall. *I Love You, But I'm Not in Love With You. Seven Steps to Saving Your Relationship*. 2006. Bloomsbury, London

7   Marshall Goldsmith with Mark Reiter. *Mojo: How to Get It, How to Keep It, How to Get It Back If You Lose It*. 2010. Hyperion, New York

Acknowledgements

I'd like to thank everyone who has helped me so far.

First of all, my wife Louisette and my colleague Ian Parlane, whose encouragement through the early drafts persuaded me that I should carry on.

Anthony Howard and Graham Wallace for their wise guidance.

Everyone at Flexible Directors, especially Trudy Gibbons for her technical input on the employment issues.

Saul Djanogly and Joan Connell for their technical input in the investment and divorce sections.

Duncan Cheatle and the members and staff at the Supper Club for their inspiration as archetypes for the 'WealthBeing cohort'.

Everyone else whose advice and wisdom I have listened to and hopefully absorbed, especially Jon Davidge, Peter Leach, Piers Denne, Charles Warner-Allen, Michael Maddison, Adrian Gilpin and Andrea Frost.

Clare Christian, Ian Shircore, Gemma Wilson and Heather Boisseau at RedDoor Publishing.

Index

Published by RedDoor

www.reddoorpublishing.com

© 2015 Malcolm Durham

The right of Malcolm Durham to be identified as author of this Work has been asserted by him in accordance with sections 77 and 78 of the Copyright, Designs and Patents Act 1988

ISBN 978-1-910453-07-0

A CIP catalogue record for this book is available from the British Library

Cover design: Clare Turner

Typesetting: Gemma Wilson

Printed by TJ International, Padstow, Cornwall